Taking *the* Field

CLARENCE & VICKY ST. JOHN

Developed by the Sunday School
Promotion & Training Department

Gospel Publishing House
Springfield, Missouri
02-0655

This is the second in a series of five books dealing with the We Build People model of discipleship. Each of the books is written to give you a deeper insight into each of the four bases of the model. The baseball diamond illustration mentioned in this book is adapted from materials developed by Pastor Rick Warren of Saddleback Church for his book *The Purpose Driven Church: Growth Without Compromising Your Message & Mission* and is used by permission of Zondervan Publishing House.

All Scripture quotations, unless otherwise indicated, are taken from the HOLY BIBLE: NEW INTERNATIONAL VERSION®; NIV®. Copyright ©1973, 1978, 1984 by International Bible Society. Used by permission of Zondervan Publishing House. All rights reserved.

©1997 by Gospel Publishing House, Springfield, Missouri 65802-1894. All rights reserved. No part of this book may be reproduced, stored in a retrieval system, or transmitted in any form or by any means—electronic, mechanical, photocopy, recording, or otherwise—without prior written permission of the copyright owner, except brief quotations used in connection with reviews in magazines or newspapers.

Library of Congress Cataloging Card Number 97-72583
International Standard Book Number 0-88243-655-4
Printed in the United States of America

Contents

Preface / 4
Introduction / 6
1. Ambassadors for Christ / 11
2. Sent to Reap / 23
3. Avenues for God's Voice / 41
4. Love in Action / 55
5. Finding the Key / 69
6. Relating to the Community / 88
7. Seeing Beyond Circumstances / 101
8. Reaching This Generation / 115

Preface

"Where do you live?" the first-century men asked Jesus. "Come and see," was His ready response.

Accepting the invitation started these two seekers on an incredible adventure that they could not have imagined.

It is always the same. Jesus calls us to come along with Him and be transformed into disciples.

What happens to the people we win through our outreaches? Do they continue to grow as mature disciples of Jesus Christ or does their spiritual development stall? Do some turn back and leave the fellowship of faith?

The church is responsible to develop the persons won through its outreach into mature disciples who will disciple others. This is the compulsion of the Great Commission. How does one become a disciple? How does a church become a disciple-making body?

Grappling with these questions gave birth to *We Build People: Making Disciples for the 21st Century*. It may be easier to understand this holistic, total-church strategy if we think of a baseball diamond with its bases and base paths. The bases are the person's commitments; the base paths, the church's.

Between home and first base the path is *include them*. The church reaches out to the disciple-to-be and seeks to win him or her for Christ. The methods may vary from the more visible ministries of the church, such as evangelistic campaigns, to the less visible, such as small-group Bible studies.

At first base the person is committed to membership, joined in relationship with Christ through salvation and to a local church through friendship. The adventure of discipleship has begun.

Between first and second base the church's role is to *instruct them*. The new believer must learn the disciplines and character of a true disciple, be established in God's Word, and develop a prayer life. He or she becomes committed to maturity.

To move developing disciples from second to third base, the church must *involve them*. Here the church helps a person identify his ministry gifts and talents and provides training and opportunities for hands-on ministry, usually under the tutelage of a mentor. The disciple is committed to ministry, finding that place in the Body for which Christ has gifted him or her.

In our definition, one truly becomes a disciple when he or she disciples others. To move people along to this point in their spiritual development, the church must *invest them*. This may include a greater role of leadership within the local church or ministry that goes beyond the church walls. The disciple is committed to mission.

Taking the Field: Reaching Out and Including the Lost is a first-base study. Clarence and Vicky St. John challenge the church to extend Jesus' invitation to the 21st-century person. By meeting needs and building relationships, the church compels the person on the fringe to come and see what Jesus offers: acceptance, belonging, and transformation.

This intentional evangelism requires us to move out of our comfort zones, engaging people who are skeptical of—often hostile to—the church. Driving our outreach and ministry efforts are values that affirm "Every person is valued and is focus of our ministry. Every person is entitled to a presentation of the gospel at his level of understanding."

Taking the Field is a study for every church leader. It is a handbook for the church that wants to be committed to including the unchurched. Writing out of a rich pastoral background, the St. Johns give practical suggestions that any church can employ to meet people's needs and build relationships that lead to discipleship.

Come and see.

Introduction

The Law of Inclusion

A church's effectiveness in evangelism and disciple-making is directly proportional to its ability to establish and cultivate meaningful relationships.

The Law of Inclusion Defined

The Law of Inclusion says: A disciple-making church intentionally provides a process that includes people in its sphere of care, causing them to desire to become believers, establishing a relationship with Jesus Christ and His body, the local church. They make a commitment to membership.

Designing Your Disciple-Making Process

The Law of Inclusion must be built into the values and culture of the church. It doesn't happen automatically. A church or ministry will ultimately turn inward and become self-serving if steps are not taken to keep its focus on including people in its circle of care and ministry.

Base 1 ministries or activities focus on *including* the unchurched and leading them to make a commitment to membership (a relationship to Jesus Christ and with the local church). These ministries should focus on including unchurched nonbelievers by (1) ministering to their needs, (2) building relationships with them, (3) including them in the group, and (4) sharing the gospel with them. These are the four habits of the Disciple-Making Process (DMP) at Base 1.

Goals of Disciples Committed to Membership

How do we know when an individual has committed to membership and that the church is effectively practicing the Law of Inclusion? The person commits to Christ and to His body, the local church, and demonstrates this commitment by a change in awareness, attitude, and action. More than just acting like a disciple, the person is becoming and developing as a true disciple of Christ.

At Base 1 true disciples should reflect the following awarenesses, attitudes, and actions in their lives.

AWARENESS GOALS

People demonstrate a commitment to membership when their *awareness* is enlightened and they know (1) what sin is and why people need a Savior; (2) that they can be saved by repenting of sin and receiving Christ as Savior and Lord; (3) that the Church is Christ's body and are compelled to fulfill the threefold mission of worship, edification, and evangelism; (4) that the Church is the family of God and that each believer is vital to the Church's mission; (5) that the Bible is the infallible, unique written revelation of God to humankind.

ATTITUDE GOALS

People demonstrate a commitment to membership when their *attitudes* reflect (1) a realization that they are sinners; (2) godly sorrow for sin and a desire to accept God's gift of salvation; (3) a desire to symbolize conversion through water baptism; (4) a recognition of the value of Christian fellowship; (5) a respect for the divinely inspired, infallible Word of God.

ACTION GOALS

People demonstrate a commitment to membership when they take *action* and (1) come to God seeking forgiveness; (2) turn from sin in repentance; (3) testify of their conversion through water baptism; (4) consistently join the fellowship of believers; (5) use the Bible to investigate claims concerning Christian faith.

Profile of Disciples Committed to Membership

What is the profile of people committed to membership? They demonstrate the characteristics of true converts. They exhibit godly sorrow for sin; they repent and accept God's gift of salvation through Jesus Christ. They testify of conversion through water baptism and evidence new life in Christ through a change in awarenesses, attitudes, and actions (see 2 Corinthians 5:17). They show love toward Jesus and hate sin. They know the Church is the family of God and begin regularly to join the fellowship of believers. They begin to value the Bible and use it to discover principles for life and living.

The inclusion phase of your Disciple-Making Process is effective when you are developing disciples that match this profile.

Resources

The following resources, intentionally focusing on salvation, are available to guide the church in helping adults make a commitment to membership:

Special Worship/Celebration/Rally Events

Adult Sunday School Classes

Radiant Life Curriculum for adults and young adults, and the Spiritual Discovery Series (Gospel Publishing House)

Support Group Ministries

For couples in second marriages and blended families; for parents of difficult children; for grief recovery; Turning Point (Teen Challenge)

Divorce Recovery Workshops and Seminars (Gospel Publishing House)

God's Design for Broken Lives—Rebuilding After Divorce (02-0344)

Divorce Care video series and study materials (28-0175)

Sequence Evangelism Seminars
(Sunday School Promotion and Training Department)

Learning To Love (714-409)
Closeness Through Communication (714-405)
Positive Parenting (714-408)
How To Talk So Your Teen Will Listen (714-406)
Managing Life's Stress (714-410)
Time and Priority Management (714-430)
How To Make Christianity Real (714-411)

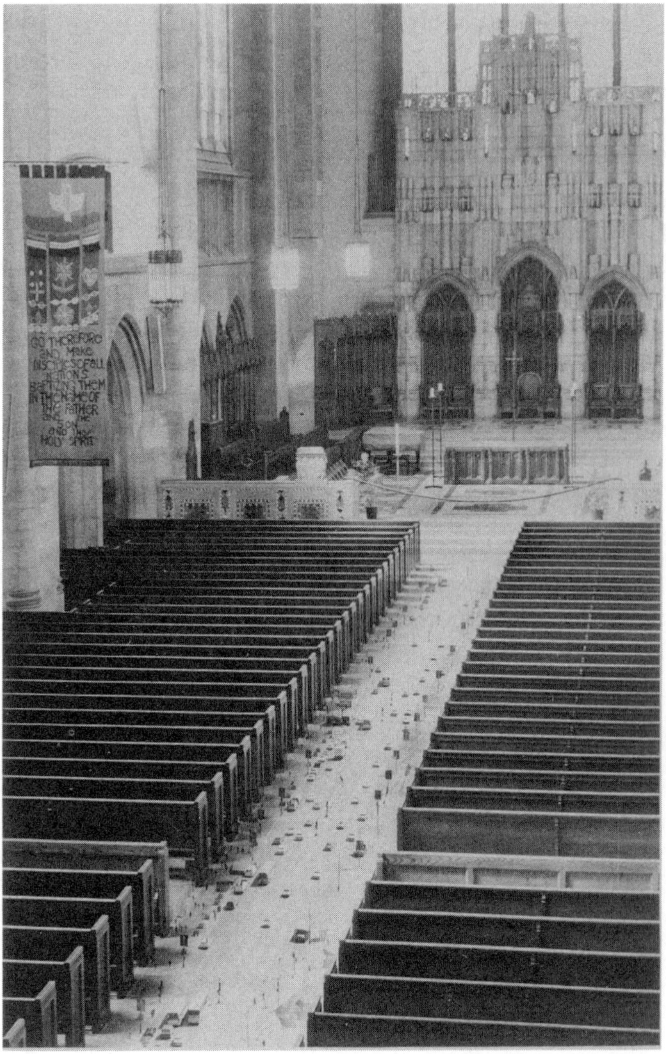

1
Ambassadors for Christ

Take a look at the photomontage by Scott Mutter on the opposite page.[1] At first glance, it appears to be the inside of a church. But if you look more closely, you will notice there are several images superimposed upon each other. The inside church front becomes the outside. The platform, or altar, area becomes the front steps of that church. The pews are the skyscrapers of the city, places where people live and work, and the aisle of the church becomes a busy city street with traffic coming and going.

This picture speaks eloquently about what our mission as a church should be: taking the church outside its walls to people who are hurting and, as a result, seeing many of them coming into the church.

The Church's Focus

The church speaks much of vision and reaching the world. However, in general, the American church has a very "inside" focus. We tend to concentrate most of our time and energy on those already in the church. As long as we, the body of Christ, remain inside the church's walls, we will have a limited impact on those outside who so desperately need what we have.

12 TAKING THE FIELD

Ministers of churches can usually be divided into two categories: Those who pastor inside the church building, tending to the church's needs and business, and those who pastor outside the walls, tending to the lost.

Every Christian also fits these two categories. Are you an inside or an outside Christian? Inside Christians, although working out in the world, concentrate their energy and focus almost entirely on the church and church activities. This would be wonderful, and permissible, if everyone in the world were in the church. Unfortunately, the majority of the world remains outside the church.

The world is not always the most pleasant of places. It can be cold, harsh, and uncaring. It can also be smothering in the heat and stench of its sin. Outside Christians strive to focus on those still in the world. This can be difficult, for the world is a rather unpleasant place where one can experience a cold shoulder from people who do not understand or accept the Christian faith.

It is comfortable, for the most part, inside our churches. Many congregations have beautiful, accommodating buildings with terrific music and great programs. Our social needs are met by Christian friends who love and accept us. With our friends we enjoy wonderful services and good fellowship.

While we have no difficulty enjoying the comforts our society provides, we can get weary of working in the world and tired of the filth that surrounds us. Christians have little in common with the ungodly. We do not like their influence on our children. Like Lot, who lived in sin-filled Sodom, we become "sick of the terrible wickedness" we see everywhere around us day after day (2 Peter 2:7,8, *The Living Bible*).

As time winds down for this world, the lines between the church and the world should become sharper and clearer—and we should hate sin and be unlike the world. The Bible warns us to "'come out from them and be separate'" (2 Corinthians 6:17) and not to be "yoked together with unbelievers" (2 Corinthians 6:14). But without love and compassion for the lost, the church becomes isolated and ineffective and loses its reason for being.

To be separate and yet love the world is a paradox. On the one hand, we are to "not love the world" (1 John 2:15), and on the other hand, we are told to "love [our] enemies" (Matthew 5:44), which is the world. We are "in this world" (1 John 4:17) but not "of the world" (John 15:19). Maintaining a balance can be difficult. Too much emphasis on one can prevent us from accomplishing the other.

We all have heard the cliché "Hate the sin, love the sinner." In our effort to be separate from the world, too often we are perceived as hating both the sin and the sinner. On the other hand, for the immature Christian, moving too close to the sinner carries the risk of being influenced and drawn away from the Lord. These dynamics need to be recognized as possibilities. Somehow we need to discover a way to walk close enough to the Lord to live above sin, yet walk close enough to sinners to influence them for Christ.

The church is reluctant to leave the safety and security of its walls, but the world is even more reluctant to come to the church. The lost are not flooding to the church except in isolated pockets of revival.

How can a church that is increasingly content to isolate itself touch a world that is resistant to the gospel? The answer to this question lies in the heart of each individual, for our actions are determined by what is in our hearts. Solomon wrote, "Above all else, guard your heart, for it is the wellspring of life" (Proverbs 4:23).

What is in our hearts? Often our hearts are filled with the cares of life, the pressing concerns for our personal and family needs. These aspects of our lives are weighty, but we cannot allow them to crowd out the more important matters of life and eternity.

God's Focus

What is on God's heart? The world—the place we often try to escape—is on God's heart. This truth is found in one of the first Scripture verses we learn as children, "'God so loved the world that he gave his one and only Son, that whoever believes in him shall not perish but have eternal life'" (John 3:16).

When we put the things that are important to God first in our lives, we find that God has a way of taking care of the other aspects of our lives. Scripture puts it this way, "'Pagans run after all these things, and your heavenly Father knows that you need them. But seek first his kingdom and his righteousness, and all these things will be given to you as well'" (Matthew 6:32,33). If we concern ourselves with the things that are important to God, He will concern himself with the things that are important to us.

Jesus' purpose in coming to this earth is clearly stated in Luke's Gospel: "'The Son of Man came to seek and to save what was lost'" (Luke 19:10). Jesus spent approximately two-thirds of His ministering situations recorded in the Gospels with people who were not committed to Him. His thrust in this world was to evangelize—to save the lost. To illustrate how He felt about the lost, Jesus told the parables of three things: the lost sheep, the lost coin, and the lost son.

In the Parable of the Lost Sheep, the Good Shepherd leaves the ninety-nine to look for the one that is lost. Scripture tells us that there is more rejoicing in heaven over one lost sinner who repents than in the ninety-nine who are safe in the church praising and worshiping God (Luke 15:3–7).

In the Parable of the Lost Coin (vv. 8–10), the woman has ten coins, but loses one. She carefully sweeps the house and searches until she finds the lost one. When she finds it, she is so excited she calls her friends and neighbors to celebrate with her.

In the Parable of the Lost Son (vv. 11–32), the father has two sons, one of whom leaves home and squanders his inheritance. The father anxiously waits and watches for his return. While the son is still a long way off, his father sees him and is "filled with compassion for him" (v. 20).

Although the father carries out the daily duties and obligations of life, his heart longs for his lost son to return home. When the lost son returns, the father puts fine robes on him, makes a feast, and celebrates his return.

When the older son comes in from the field, he hears music and dancing. He learns from a servant that his wayward brother is home again, and everyone is celebrating. The elder brother displays an attitude often found in the church—he is concerned about himself first. He becomes angry and refuses to go in and join the celebration.

When his father comes out and pleads with him to come in, his answer shows he felt justified in his attitude and anger. He said, "'All these years I've been slaving for you and never disobeyed your orders. Yet you never gave me even a young goat so I could celebrate with my friends. But when this son of yours who has squandered your property with prostitutes comes home, you kill the fattened calf for him'" (vv. 25–30).

The focus in these three parables is on the one lost, not on those already found (Luke 15:31,32). Scripture reveals that God desires us to have the same focus. Jesus came to earth to save the lost, and He states clearly what His desire is for us: "'As the Father has sent me, I am sending you'" (John 20:21). Jesus came with a reason—to focus on the lost. "God was reconciling the world to himself in Christ, not counting men's sins against them. And he has committed to us the message of reconciliation. *We are therefore Christ's ambassadors,* as though God were making His appeal through us. We implore you on Christ's behalf: Be reconciled to God" (2 Corinthians 5:19,20, emphasis added).

As this Scripture passage reminds us, we are Christ's ambassadors, His representatives to the lost people of this world.

Christ's Ambassadors

Ambassadors are representatives of their home country, stationed in every major foreign country of the world. The primary duty of ambassadors is to represent their country and their country's interests in their assigned country. The embassy building out of which a foreign ambassador operates serves as a refuge, or safe zone, for fellow countrymen living or traveling in that area should the need arise. It also serves as a resource center, providing information for those who may need help in dealing with a different culture.

Christians are citizens of heaven; in essence, we are ambassadors to earth. In a sense the church operates as an embassy in every community, serving as a refuge and resource center for the believer.

RECOGNIZING THE CULTURE

Good ambassadors recognize that the culture of the land they are assigned to is not the same as that of their home country.

Often we fail to realize that as Christians we are living in an alien culture. Our values and perceptions are not always liked or understood. Christians are a subculture, a culture within a culture. We even have our own language—words and terms that are foreign to the culture of this world.

Perhaps you have heard the story of the man who went to the Saturday morning evangelism class his church was conducting. He became so excited about winning his world for Christ that he decided he'd try his skills out right away. A little hesitant to share his faith with people he knew, he headed out of town. After driving a few moments, he spied a farmer working near the side of the road. So he stopped and nervously asked the farmer, "Are you lost?"

The farmer looked at him a moment and replied, "Nope, lived here all my life."

Not quite knowing what to do next, the man asked, "Well, are you folks Christians?"

The farmer looked like he was comprehending and answered, "Oh, Christians! They live down the road about three miles."

Thinking he should probably give it one more stab, the man asked, "Are you ready for the Rapture to take place?"

The farmer asked, "Rapture? When's that gonna happen?"

Feeling like he was making some headway finally, the man

replied, "We don't know. Maybe today, maybe tomorrow, maybe the next day."

The farmer said, "Well, don't tell my wife. She'll want to go all three days."

This story illustrates how our Christian jargon often does not penetrate the mind of the unchurched. In fact, this is one of the major reasons the unchurched turn off the church. Some examples of phrases Christians often use include "Be covered by the blood of the Lamb," "Be fed by the Word," "Possess a broken spirit," "Pursue a Christian walk," and "Seek the fellowship of the Holy Spirit."

These are wonderful scriptural concepts that mean a great deal to us, but they are a foreign language that needs interpretation if they are to be understood by those unfamiliar with the church. Author and master poll-taker George Barna states we often fail "because well-intentioned Christians have used impenetrable language and concepts to tell nonbelievers about the world's greatest gift. . . . What we communicate to people using these words and phrases is that if they don't speak the secret language, they can't be part of the special club. When we use Churchspeak or Christianese, we alienate rather than enlighten people."[2]

Although Paul was dealing with the operation of the gifts of the Spirit within public church services, he laid out a communication principle that can be applied to this culture-within-a-culture concept: "Unless you speak intelligible words with your tongue, how will anyone know what you are saying? You will just be speaking into the air. Undoubtedly there are all sorts of languages in the world, yet none of them is without meaning. If then I do not grasp the meaning of what someone is saying, I am a foreigner to the speaker, and he is a foreigner to me" (1 Corinthians 14:9–11).

UNDERSTANDING THE LANGUAGE

Good ambassadors seek to understand the culture and the language of the land in which they are assigned to live.

18 TAKING THE FIELD

Understanding the language allows communication to take place. Understanding the culture helps to minimize misunderstandings. Understanding is the key to being understood.

To be effective, ambassadors need to understand how situations and words may be perceived by the people of the country where they are living. What may be meaningless to ambassadors' backgrounds may be totally misunderstood and offensive to the culture they are trying to relate to. Rather than seeking to be understood, ambassadors should seek to understand.

When missionaries apply for overseas ministry, everything possible is done to prepare them for life in another culture. Every missionary has a humorous story or two to tell of their early experiences with a foreign culture and language. They sincerely thought they were communicating some truth, but the people listening understood something entirely different.

Calvin Olson, a veteran missionary to Bangladesh, tells of the first sermon he preached in the Bengali language. He was speaking from John 8:12 where Jesus said, "'I am the light of the world.'" However, the Bengali word for "light'" was very similar to another word in their language. What the people listening heard him say was, "I am the potato of the world."

In another situation, standing by the native pastor at the door, Olson heard the pastor repeat the same phrase to each person leaving the church. The pastor shook hands and said to his parishioners, "May God bless you." Thinking he was repeating what the pastor was saying, Olson also greeted everyone in the same manner. However, his words to the congregation were, "May God put you in jail."

Mistakes may not be avoidable, but the good ambassador seeks to understand the language and the culture in order to prevent further misunderstandings or offenses.

PRESENTING GOD'S INTERESTS

Good ambassadors seek the most effective way to present their country's interests.

Ambassadors try to present the interests of their country to a people who may not understand their country's values, concepts, or interests and, furthermore, may not even care. Good ambassadors seek to minimize misunderstandings.

Another missionary tells of printing brochures for distribution, using the picture that we often see of Jesus with His hand raised. However, just prior to printing the brochures, someone noticed that it was the left hand of Jesus that was raised. In our culture it makes little difference which hand is lifted in greeting, but in many cultures the left hand is a hand of offense. Sending out that material in that culture would have caused a needless barrier to their reception of the gospel. The solution to this problem was to turn the negative. This minor adjustment made the material acceptable to that culture. The message was not changed; only the way that the message was presented was changed.

We need to think about how we are presenting Christ's interests. We may need to adjust some areas that would make us more effective in reaching the culture in which we live. Adjusting our presentation does not involve compromising the message. It involves recognizing the needless barriers the church sometimes erects that make it difficult for people to respond to the gospel. These barriers are rarely erected deliberately. They are put up unintentionally because we do not understand how we are being perceived.

"User friendly" is a description that has been added to our language with the advent of computers. To sell personal computers to a greater number of buyers, it was necessary to make them easy to use—user friendly. Some people have taken the concept of being "seeker friendly" to the extreme of changing their message to what they think unbelievers want to hear in order to bring them into the church. Others suggest that we should be "seeker aware"—being more conscious of their needs.

Perhaps individual Christians and the Church as a whole should take this awareness a step farther and become "world aware," then "world wise." We should become aware of how the world perceives us, but we should also be aware of the things that we may be saying and doing that are being misunderstood and misinterpreted. Then we should be wise enough to make the appropriate adjustments to accommodate the world's understanding of God's interests.

Little areas that have nothing to do with the message itself can have everything to do with how that message is received; for example, the Christian who leaves a tract at a restaurant with little or no tip. Granted, God can do anything and He may perform a miracle to make that tract effective. In general, however, that tract reinforces a negative stereotype of Christians who are cheap, out of touch, and concerned only with getting their view across. Perhaps leaving a tip above the 15 percent of the bill might increase the chance of the tract's effectiveness. A kind, friendly manner and a generous tip (particularly in places you frequent often and are well-known) would probably be the most effective witness of all.

Christians who are thoughtless and demanding (especially in an establishment that is well aware a particular church is being represented) foster a negative feeling toward God. Christians are always representing the church and, more importantly, representing the Lord. The world is watching and making judgments regarding us and what we represent.

Some years ago a young man showed up at the church we were pastoring. In the course of conversation with him, I asked him what brought him to our church.

He began, "I often waited on your family when you came into Pizza Hut. When you came in, we would fight over who would get to serve you, because you always gave a big tip."

Though this had been his only connection with our church, when he came to a difficult period in his life and was seeking some answers, he walked into our church based on the conclusions he drew from our manner and especially because of our tips. This young man ended up attending Bible college to prepare for ministry.

Our lives powerfully influence people even when we are unaware of it. It is frightening to realize that our careless attitudes and actions can cause people to step farther away from God.

What changes of attitudes do we need to make? What needless wrong perceptions may we be giving to people? We must answer these questions as individuals. The answers will vary from year to year, community to community, and individual to individual. They depend to some extent upon the events taking place in our complex world.

Be aware of what is currently happening in our world, and be sensitive to what is being wrongly perceived about Christianity in general. Then, make an effort not to deliberately add to that wrong perception, and take the steps necessary to change any actions or attitudes that may be reinforcing that view. Successful evangelism often takes place when we find out what we are doing wrong and take steps to stop it.

We cannot remove all opposition; there will always be some resistance to the things of God. Even when everything is done with the best of intentions and the utmost care, the message can still be misunderstood. Jesus was not always understood by the world. However, that is no excuse for Christ's ambassadors to go blindly ahead, allowing their message to be needlessly misunderstood. We must present God's interests in the best way possible.

CULTIVATING RELATIONSHIPS

Good ambassadors recognize the importance of cultivating relationships with people in their assigned country. If people like us and respect us, they are more likely to respond to our message. We are not likely to positively influence someone for Christ who doesn't like us.

Pioneers who took the gospel to pagan cultures were heroes who often went to hard and hostile unreached areas. In those instances where they encountered a strong resistance to the gospel, they would go to unusual lengths to communicate clearly and to win the hearts of the people. Sometimes they would pay for their efforts with their lives.

Only as the barriers of resistance to the gospel are torn down and as trust and respect take their place are people won to Christ. This is true in all cultures. We win people to ourselves first.

The major part of the success of any ministry is getting along with people. People will help you succeed if they like you. They will even cover your mistakes. But if they do not like you, they will sabotage even the good work that you do. "The impact of a message often depends on who says it."[3]

"If we like someone we will more likely listen to him, if we don't like him we will most likely not listen to him. And if we dislike someone strongly enough, no matter what he says, we will probably be opposed to it."[4]

Jesus was a master at relating to people. "Jesus grew in wisdom and stature, and in favor with God and men" (Luke 2:52). "Jesus . . . went around doing good" (Acts 10:38), and "The large crowd listened to him with delight" (Mark 12:37). The first church enjoyed "the favor of all the people" (Acts 2:47).

Christ's ambassadors seek first to understand the culture they are ministering in and then seek to be understood in order to effectively present God's interests.

Endnotes

[1] Scott Mutter, *Surrational Images* (Corte Madera, Calif.: Portal Publications, 1993).

[2] George Barna, *Evangelism That Works* (Ventura, Calif.: Regal Books, 1995), 41–42.

[3] Alan Dollar, quoted in Dick Innes, *I Hate Witnessing,* (Ventura, Calif.: Vision House, 1983), 38.

[4] Dick Innes, *I Hate Witnessing,* 39.

2
Sent to Reap

People have many dreams and goals. Sports enthusiasts dream of playing on a great ball team, playing in a state tournament, or having the opportunity to play college football. Dreams of great successes are common for the average boy. But, as a 14-year-old sitting on the back row of the church, I sensed God calling and placing a greater dream—His dream—in my heart. That dream was to someday pioneer a church. It was awesome to think that God would want to use me. I was from one of the poorest families in town. And yet, God chose me. It was an overwhelming thought.

I am so thankful for the person who came to my hometown and started an Assemblies of God church. My father was an alcoholic, and my mother was a strong, stubborn German. After having four children and enduring my father's drinking problems, she told him, "If you drink again, don't come home."

Somehow, my dad realized that she meant what she said. In desperation, he went to my Baptist uncle and asked, "What shall I do?"

My uncle replied, "If I were you, I'd go down to that Assemblies of God church. They believe in deliverance."

On a Sunday evening 10 days later my father followed that

advice and walked down the aisle in response to the altar call. That trip to the altar changed our family forever. Instead of divorcing, my parents were married for 54 years. They established a Christian home into which I was born a couple of years later.

I remember sitting in that same small church as a 14-year-old, now sensing God's call upon my life, and watching it shrink from 100 people to 40. We had been told our church had the best message and the most power. I believed that then and still believe it today. Yet, even at that young age, it was hard to understand. If this truly was the best message for the lost, why was that particular church on such a downward slide?

This is what had happened to that church in that community. An initial revival resulted in a group of people forming the nucleus of a new church. Friends and family members joined that group. After a period of time, the church was able to support a pastor, had capable leaders serving in the various departments, and settled into a comfortable routine. Increasingly, members became more content in their church and at the same time more isolated from their community. Church attendance leveled off. Then natural attrition took place as people moved away and a few problems developed in the church. Because no significant way of reaching new people had been developed, the church began its downward slide.

In one study an interesting process in the life of a church was discovered: 20 years of growth, 20 years of leveling off, 20 years of decline. This study illustrates the process that had gone on in my home church. If new people are not added and folded into a church and its leadership, the church plateaus for a time then begins to decline.

The good news is that this does not have to happen. All across America are churches that were able to interrupt either the leveling-off process or the declining process. They were able to make the necessary changes and are thriving once again.

If a farmer does not have a crop for one or two years, he may be able to hang on with some type of assistance program. But

Average Life Cycle Of a Church

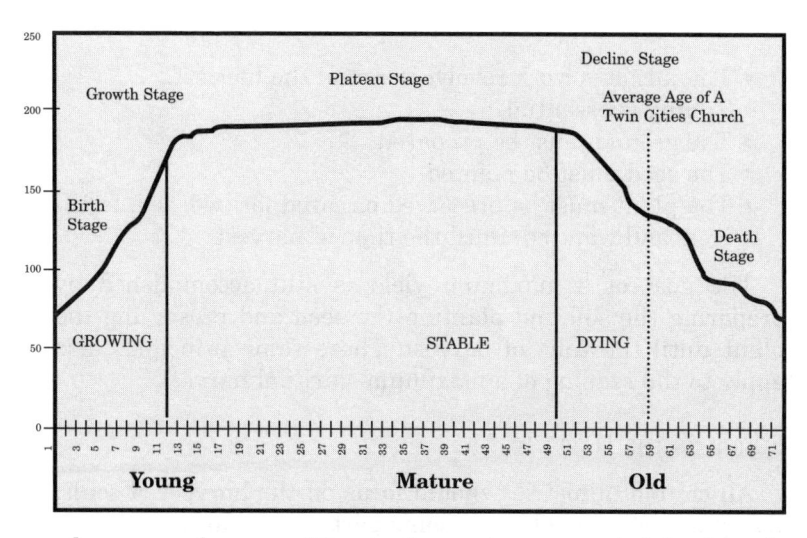

when several years without a harvest are repeated, bankruptcy is inevitable. The church, likewise, must have a continual influx of new converts to survive, for the church is always one generation away from extinction.

When Jesus taught about our responsibility to the lost, He often used illustrations easily understood by the agriculture-based society of His day: "'The harvest is plentiful'" (Luke 10:2); "'I sent you to reap'" (John 4:38). Although the urbanization of America has made the farming process less familiar to a good portion of our society, most people still understand this terminology.

Timeless Principles of the Harvest

Principles governing the harvest were set in motion at creation. They were true in Jesus' day, are true today, and will be true tomorrow. "'As long as the earth endures, seedtime and harvest, cold and heat, summer and winter, day and night will never cease'" (Genesis 8:22).

Although methods of farming have changed and vastly improved over the years, the basic format remains the same:

- The farmer's work revolves around the harvest.
- Timing is essential.
- The ground must be prepared.
- The seed must be planted.
- The plant must be preserved or cared for (weeded, fertilized, and watered) until the time of harvest.

The goal of a maximum yield is still accomplished by preparing the soil and planting the seed and preserving the plant until the time of harvest. These same principles also apply to the reaping of a maximum spiritual harvest.

FOCUS ON THE HARVEST

All church ministries should focus on the harvest of souls. Every ministry should play some part in the harvest process. Some activities may serve the purpose of preparing the ground. Some may be designed to plant the seed of the gospel in an individual's life. Some may water and nourish the growing plant. And some may be designed to actually bring in the harvest.

RECOGNIZE TIMING

The harvester recognizes the importance of timing. First, the fields are plowed and prepared for planting. Then, at the proper time, the seed is planted. The seedling is nurtured carefully. At appropriate times, it is watered, weeded, and fertilized. And, finally, the time comes for the harvest to be gathered. "There is a time for everything, and a season for every activity under heaven: . . . a time to plant and a time to uproot" (Ecclesiastes 3:1,2).

Timing is also important for a spiritual harvest. There is "a time to be silent and a time to speak" (Ecclesiastes 3:7). The timing of what we may say to the lost when directed by the Holy Spirit is described by the writer of Proverbs: "How good is a timely word!" (15:23).

There are appropriate times for all types of harvest work, from the low-key approach of just living a Christian life before the lost to that of actually harvesting the crop by leading a person to salvation and to live for God. We need wisdom to understand God's timing.

Prepare the Ground

The ground must be prepared. Whole technologies are based on the proper preparation of the soil for its intended crop. Experts can test the soil, tell you what nutrients are needed, and what type of seed will produce the best harvest.

Likewise, much information is available to the church. Statistics can provide clues to what is lacking in the soil of our communities and of individual lives. Scripture identifies four types of soil: wayside (hard), rocky, thorny, and good (Luke 8:5–8).

Some ground is soft and ready for planting. It requires little work. Other ground has, for a variety of reasons, become hardened and will take longer to prepare. Some ground may have to be cleared of barriers, such as trees and rocks, before a crop can be planted.

We all would like to have the good ground to work with. It is wonderful when people respond quickly and are added to our churches with a minimum amount of effort. Unfortunately, many of us are placed in fields where the ground is hard and resistant to the gospel seed. This resistance can be caused by many things:

- People's sinful nature and resulting lifestyle, which is hostile to God.
- Cares, riches, and pleasures of this life. Jesus identified these as primary preventers of the seed taking root and growing to maturity (Luke 8:14).
- Misconceptions or negative stereotypes of Christianity.

These are often reinforced by the media, and sometimes by careless or overzealous, unbalanced Christians. We are often our own worst enemy.
- Failures of Christian leaders. David received punishment after his sin with Bathsheba because by his deed he had "made the enemies of the Lord show utter contempt" (2 Samuel 12:14).

These are just a few factors that can harden people so they do not easily receive the seed. But even rocky, thorny, or hard ground can become good ground if enough care is given to it. We can add nutrients of love, care, and concern that will help soften the soil and give the seed of the gospel a better chance to take root and grow.

PLANT THE SEED

Although some natural seeding takes place (seeds are scattered by the wind), we would all starve if not for farmers' deliberate planting. The seed must be planted. According to Romans 1:20, a natural recognition of God is built into every person's heart. This natural seeding alone causes a few people to turn to Christ. However, planting the seed of the gospel through Christians' deliberate involvement with individuals and communities will produce a more bountiful harvest. Seed that is planted in the right season, in the right way, has the best chance of producing a plentiful harvest.

Just as the farmer can do certain things to increase the harvest in the natural world, so the Christian can set in motion, through prayer and action, things that will increase the chances of a spiritual harvest.

CARE FOR THE SEED

The seed must be cared for to ensure a maximum harvest. In the farming areas of our nation are huge irrigation systems that water the fields. The farmer does all he can to ensure that the seed comes to maturity. The crop is not only watered, but also weeded, fertilized, and sprayed with pesticides. All this is done at appropriate times to preserve the seed and the plant until the time of harvest.

Just as certain nutrients are added to the ground to assist the various soil types, so different people respond to the gospel in different ways. God deals with each of us as individuals.

HARVEST THE CROP

At the proper time the crop is harvested. Today's farming methods differ vastly from those of years gone by. It is still possible in many third-world countries to observe farming being done in the same manner as it was centuries ago. However, in developed countries, the farmer has the latest equipment and technology to help him obtain the largest crop possible. Yet, for all the different methods used throughout the years, the basic process of farming and the goal of reaping the harvest remain the same.

Just as the farming process has changed but the goal of reaping is the same, bringing people to Jesus remains the same. Only the process or methods of doing so have changed.

Laws of the Harvest

A successful farmer understands the process of preparing, planting, and nurturing that leads to a plentiful harvest. He also understands the laws of the harvest.

REAP WHAT WAS SOWN

All life comes from former life; there is no such thing as spontaneous generation. We reap only what was planted, either naturally or purposely—by God or by people—for either positive or negative results.

History records that the Church has enjoyed great harvest times, times when revival occurred and virtually whole towns came to Christ. Times of harvest do not just happen. Often a local church or individuals can be pinpointed who gave themselves to months or years of earnest prayer. Even where revival seemingly comes out of nowhere, someone, somewhere, did the preparation work.

A few years ago an intercessor felt he should fast and pray for 30 days for Albania to open up to the gospel. Soon after he finished his fast, that country opened to the gospel. It is always amazing to pray and then see Christian influences move in as God begins to work from many different directions for that request.

In the process of sowing and reaping, we often have the joy of reaping what others sowed. What Jesus said to His disciples is still true today: "'I sent you to reap what you have not worked for. Others have done the hard work, and you have reaped the benefits of their labor'" (John 4:38). Paul acknowledges that others may help in the harvest of what we've sown. He said, "I planted the seed, Apollos watered it, but God made it grow" (1 Corinthians 3:6).

At times we prepare the ground in a person's life, someone else sows the seed, another waters that seed, and still another reaps the harvest. Our job is to cooperate with God and do our part in the process, whether it is preparing the ground, sowing the seed, watering and fertilizing the plant, or reaping the harvest.

REAP IN KIND

Have you heard the saying "What goes around, comes around"? That's another way of saying we will reap the kind of things we sow. If we sow corn, we will not reap beans; we will reap corn. Whatever is sown will be reaped. Therefore, if we sow good thoughts and actions, we will reap good from those good thoughts and actions. If we sow evil, we will reap a harvest of evil (Proverbs 22:8).

We need to be continually involved in some part of the harvest process. Some churches and Christians spend no time working the soil (developing relationships), sowing the seed (speaking about God), or nurturing the seed (caring for the lost). Then they wonder why they never reap a harvest. The apostle Paul tells us why with this law that is so familiar to farmers: "A man reaps what he sows" (Galatians 6:7).

REAP IN SEASON

We do not see immediate results from our sowing. No harvest comes immediately after the seed is planted. It must await God's appointed time. Every crop has a different growing season. Some crops develop in the cool spring weather and are harvested before the hot summer sun arrives. Other crops need the heat of the sun. The seeds are planted in soil that has been prepared, then with care, rain, sunshine, and warm temperatures, the seeds germinate and grow to maturity for harvesting. Some plants grow almost overnight; others, such as trees, take many years of changing seasons to reach maturity.

In the same manner, every individual and every community is different. Some are soon spiritually ready for salvation. Others take a lot of nurturing and encouraging through several seasons. But when the season is right for them, they sprout and grow to maturity. We sow in one season and reap in another.

REAP AN INCREASE

The harvest is greater than the seed planted. We reap more than we sow. If this were not the case, no farmer would plant anything. One kernel of corn can produce several ears with many kernels on them. A person may bring one other person to the Lord, then that other person may be the means of winning hundreds of lost people to the Lord. When we sow good, we bountifully receive from God, who is debtor to no one. Eternity alone will reveal the complete results of our sowing seeds of righteousness.

No fact is more significant and sobering than the fact that

those who sow seeds of evil also receive an increase. "'They sow the wind and they reap the whirlwind'" (Hosea 8:7).

Reap in Proportion

Even though one kernel of corn may produce several ears, each with many kernels, to sow only one kernel severely limits how many ears and subsequent kernels of corn will be harvested. That is a natural law that the apostle Paul referred to when he said, "Whoever sows sparingly will also reap sparingly, and whoever sows generously will also reap generously" (2 Corinthians 9:6).

We reap in proportion to what we sow. The more ground we cover and the more seeds we sow, the more likely that many of them will germinate, and the greater the harvest will be. It's also logical that the more people we tell about God, the greater the likelihood that, through our multiplied efforts, more than one person will be persuaded to believe in Jesus.

Reap by Perseverance

It's interesting that evil comes to harvest on its own. It needs no nurturing or special care by a gardener. Like evil, weeds grow by themselves without special attention. This is not true of vegetables; they require patient care and nurturing.

A spiritual harvest differs from a natural harvest in this regard: Once the seed has been planted, we know it will mature by the harvest season. When a spiritual seed is sown, we do not know how long it will take to mature. Therefore, waiting for the spiritual harvest in an individual's life can be hard and discouraging. That is why Scripture tells us, "Let us not become weary in doing good, for at the proper time we will reap a harvest if we do not give up" (Galatians 6:9).

The spiritual harvest will come. It will take patience, determination, and effort on our part, but a good harvest is worth the perseverance.

REAP THE CURRENT CROP

Last year is a fact of history that cannot be relived. Failure to get the seeds sown before the spring rains or to harvest the crop before it is too ripe cannot be undone. We can do nothing about last year's harvest; we can do nothing to change it. Our concern should be about what we are producing right now.

We can do something about the crop we want to harvest this year. We can make sure we don't make the same mistakes we did last year. We can do research to learn how to be more productive. Then we can practice some of the improved methods and work smarter toward a greater harvest.

We must learn from the past, then put it behind us. We cannot undo our failures, and we must not stop because of them. We cannot give up. Every believer can have a part in the harvest. We need to be involved in some part of the church's harvest process. We must prepare the ground and sow the seed now if we expect to reap a harvest at some time in the future.

Workers Sent to the Harvest

Finally, the long-awaited time for harvest takes place. Harvesting crews work their way from state to state and from crop to crop. When the crop is ready, it must be harvested; it does not wait for the harvesters to prepare. They must harvest the crop at the peak time for the optimum produce. That part of the farming process has not changed over time—the crop must be harvested when it is ready. That means the farmer must have workers to send into the field when it is ripe.

"SENT ONES"

Jesus said, "'The harvest is plentiful but the workers are few. Ask the Lord of the harvest, therefore, to send out workers into his harvest field'" (Matthew 9:37). There is no question about whether you are sent. That was settled long ago. When you became a Christian, you became a "sent one." Every

Christian is sent to the harvest. Jesus said, "'As the Father has sent me, I am sending you'" (John 20:21).

From the beginning, God has been in the sending business.

- God chose Abraham and sent him to a new country to establish a nation that would be called the people of God (Genesis 12).
- God sent Joseph to Egypt to influence Pharaoh and preserve Joseph's family from famine (Genesis 37 through 50).
- God sent Moses to free His chosen people from slavery to another Pharaoh and to bring them to the Promised Land (Exodus 3).
- God sent David to kill the giant Goliath, who had been troubling Israel, then on to become Israel's greatest king (1 Samuel 17 through 24).
- God sent Esther to become a queen who would then influence her husband and save the Jewish people (Esther 4 through 5).
- God sent Jeremiah as a prophet to the nations (Jeremiah 1:5).
- God sent Daniel to represent Him before pagan kings and a pagan nation (Daniel 1 through 3).
- God sent Paul and Peter to the Gentiles (Acts 9:15; 10,11).
- God sent Matthew to the Jewish people.
- God sent Mark to the Romans.
- God sent Luke to the Greeks.

The harvesters are not called unless there is a crop to harvest. When Jesus said, "Go," He had someone in mind for us to reap. "'The field is the world'" (Matthew 13:38), and we are each responsible for our portion of that field.

What is in our field? Primarily, it includes family, friends, neighbors, and people we associate with daily. Any place of influence God puts us in is a part of our field. Every person is either a mission field or a missionary.

As sent ones, we fall into one of two categories according to Scripture: faithful or unfaithful. Faithful laborers are true to their responsibilities, using the talents and the abilities given to them. They will not be judged on the amount of their harvest, but on their faithfulness.

Jesus told a parable to illustrate the two categories. He said a landowner who was going to a distant country called his servants and gave each of them money to invest for him while he was gone. After a time, he returned and called his servants to him again. Two of them had doubled the money he gave them (Luke 19:12–19). They were faithful servants, using what he gave them as he told them to do. He praised them, calling them "good and faithful servants" for what they did with what he gave them. Then he gave them greater responsibilities to reward them for their faithfulness.

The unfaithful servant was also given money to invest, but he hid it and did not use it for his master (Luke 19:20–23). The unfaithful laborers in the field are those who refuse to use the abilities given them to help with the harvest. When the farmer returns, they will be condemned for their unfaithfulness just as this servant was (v. 26). They will receive no reward, and what they were given will be taken away.

GOD'S PURPOSES

We are sent for God's purposes. God could have chosen to win the world by using angels. Although there are instances where angels have appeared to people with a message, in the majority of cases He has chosen to use people to deliver His message.

God orchestrates time and events. He told Jeremiah, "'Before I formed you in the womb I knew you, before you were born I set you apart; I appointed you as a prophet to the nations'" (Jeremiah 1:5). He also knew us before we were born, and He has placed us in our families and in our communities at this particular time in history for His divine purposes.

Sometimes I hear the complaint, "I am so sick of this job [or this neighborhood, or this school]. I am the only one who is a Christian. I can hardly take it. Pray for me."

My response is always, "Praise God! You are on a divine appointment. There were no Christians there before God placed you there. God thought enough of you to allow you to be a light for Him in a dark place."

We are chosen, called, and placed where we are for His divine purposes. You may say, "I did not feel any special call to this place, or this town, and I certainly didn't choose my family. This is just the way circumstances are for me."

Generally, we should live out God's will in the place where He saved us unless divinely directed otherwise. "Each one should remain in the situation which he was in when God called him" (1 Corinthians 7:20). These verses lead us to believe that the family we are in and the town and state we live in are where God desires to use us.

Truly believing that we are where God wants us would revolutionize our lives! We would start looking at our lives from a different perspective: God has a purpose for me in this town. God has a purpose for me in this family. God has a purpose for me in this neighborhood. God has a purpose for me in this school or this job. An ambassador to this strategic neighborhood and this city was needed, and God thought enough of me to place me here. If He thought someone else could do a better job, then that person would be here instead.

We are God's man or woman, in God's place and in God's time, to accomplish God's purposes.

Our Own Need

We are sent or placed where we are for our own need, our own benefit. Whether we realize it or not, we are created with the need to have a sense of purpose or worth, a reason for being.

All people have a desire to find meaning in their lives and to make a difference in this world. This desire is often distorted by Satan and misplaced on things, power, or success. People leave homes, marriages, and jobs, seeking fulfillment or satisfaction, hoping to gain that sense of accomplishment. We all want our lives to count for something. People in deep depression, some of whom end their lives by suicide, often voice these questions: "What purpose is there for my life? What is the use of all of this? Why am I worthless, useless, of no value?"

The desire for meaning in life can be truly satisfied in people's lives only when they grasp the sense of purpose that God alone can give—the same sense of destiny that Esther must have had when Mordecai said to her, "'Who knows but that you have come to royal position for such a time as this?'" (Esther 4:14).

Happiness and fulfillment come to those who know that they are where they are supposed to be and that they are there for a purpose. God calls and sends us for our own benefit.

OTHER BELIEVERS' NEEDS

We are sent for each other. When we come to Christ for salvation, we become part of the body of Christ, which consists of all true believers. We also become part of a local body of believers with a place and responsibility in a local church. Each believer has gifts that are to be contributed and used in that body (Ephesians 4:16). We are needed to do our part in the body of Christ. Whether we are a visible part, such as an eye or a mouth or a right hand, or whether we are unseen, like the heart or the kidney or even the little toe, we are important to the well-being of the body. While our function in the body helps it to perform as it should, just being there in our place to do our part can inspire others to be faithful in their functions also.

THE WORLD'S NEED

We are sent for the world's sake. We are not here for just ourselves. God loved this world so much that He gave His only Son to redeem it (John 3:16). This is the harvest field where we are placed to be faithful servants, using the abilities the Master has given us till He returns.

Although the world does a nice packaging job, making things look nice on the surface, we live in a broken, hurting place. Some of us live in nice, manicured neighborhoods that paint a pretty picture of society. But scratching the surface of that cultured neighborhood reveals heartache, worry, and uncertainty beneath the shine and glitter. Others live in urban areas where the needs of broken hearts, broken families, and broken lives are right out in the open.

Jesus said that He was sending us just as His Father sent Him. Wherever people live, it is a community of people God loves. He has placed us in our communities for the sake of those people who have broken hearts and lives and are slaves to sin. It is a better place because we are there.

The Message

We are sent to deliver a message. Long ago Isaiah wrote words that were later quoted by Jesus in Luke's Gospel: "The Spirit of the Sovereign Lord is on me, because the Lord has anointed me to preach good news to the poor. He has sent me to bind up the brokenhearted, to proclaim freedom for the captives and release from darkness for the prisoners, to proclaim the year of the Lord's favor and the day of vengeance of our God, to comfort all who mourn, and provide for those who grieve in Zion—to bestow on them a crown of beauty instead of ashes, the oil of gladness instead of mourning, and a garment of praise instead of a spirit of despair" (Isaiah 61:1–3).

Look at the elements to be contained in our message:

- Good tidings to the meek
- The binding up of the brokenhearted
- Freedom for the captives
- The release of darkness for the prisoners
- The proclamation the acceptable year of the Lord, the day of vengeance of our God

- Comfort to all who mourn
- A crown of beauty instead of ashes
- Oil of joy for mourning
- The garment of praise for the spirit of despair

Look at the list. *We can give those things!* We can help bind up the brokenhearted person by listening, caring, and being there.

When a friend is being held captive or bound by some fear, habit, or circumstance, we can bring hope for liberty.

We can proclaim that God is concerned about where the person is right now. We can tell all the good things the Lord has done for us and wants to do for others.

When a friend's life seems to have crumbled to ashes, we can be there to listen, support, pray, and bring beauty to replace the ashes.

And we can help those in grief by being concerned and understanding and by pointing them to a Source of strength greater than they are—to a Rock they can hold on to in difficult times.

All of the actions above are within the capabilities of the newest and least-trained Christian. These actions should automatically spring out of a heart of love for others.

Our message must be lived out by our actions. The old adage "Your actions speak so loud I cannot hear what you are saying" certainly holds true for the Christian in today's society. If we want people to listen when we speak, then we must earn the right to be heard. We should be the first to give a word of encouragement or consolation to the hurting or to bring a dish of food to the person in need in our neighborhood. Not only should our personal lives incorporate these values, but our classes and ministries should do so also.

When the individual and the church cooperate in carrying out these objectives, they will lift up, bind up, liberate, inform, comfort, renew, and cause rejoicing. We can do it! We are sent to reap for the Master. We have the message of hope people need.

OUR ACCOUNTABILITY

We will be held accountable for carrying God's message of love to the lost world around us. With every privilege comes an even greater responsibility. This is serious business. God loves the world so much and believes in us enough to trust us with oversight of a portion of His field. Our portion of the field, as mentioned before, includes our family, friends, people we have influence over, and any ministries we may be involved in, such as teaching.

Like any giver of responsibility, God demands faithfulness on our part. "Not many of you should presume to be teachers, my brothers, because you know that we who teach will be judged more strictly" (James 3:1). Fortunately, He does not leave us without tools. He places us in specific areas, gives us the message He wants delivered through our lives, and then works alongside us to help us accomplish our task. We are not sent out alone.

3
Avenues for God's Voice

Have you had God speak to you? Few people have heard the audible voice of God, but Jesus said, "'No one can come to me unless the Father who sent me draws him. . . . Everyone who listens to the Father and learns from him comes to me'" (John 6:44–45). We have all heard His voice or we could not have come to Christ.

God's Voice to Believers

Jesus used a common example in describing His relationship to His people: the shepherd and his sheep. He said the sheep listen to the voice of the shepherd. The shepherd "'calls his own sheep by name and leads them out. When he has brought out all his own, he goes on ahead of them, and his sheep follow him because they know his voice'" (John 10:3–4).

How do individuals hear God's voice? He speaks in many ways, but primarily He speaks through His Word. Every day we have the opportunity of picking up the Scriptures and letting God speak to us. As we go through the daily routine of life, we sense, or are impressed by, the prompting of the Holy Spirit. He reminds us of Bible teaching we've heard (John

14:26). He leads us into truth (John 16:13). He corrects, instructs, rebukes, and trains us in righteousness through God's Word (2 Timothy 3:16). These impressions by the Holy Spirit are always in accordance with and reinforcement of the Word of God. At times, God speaks to us through our circumstances as doors open and shut in our lives. God also speaks to us through our times in prayer.

How does God speak to the church body? He speaks to the body of Christ in many ways: through the preaching and teaching of the Word, through the gifts of the Spirit operating when the Church meets together, and through the counsel of godly people.

When God speaks to believers, He speaks in terms we can understand. We have the choice to listen and obey the voice of God or to ignore Him.

Missing the Voice of God

If we look back in history, we see that God's people often had difficulty understanding what God was saying. This was not because God did not speak clearly. He made His message plain, but something interfered with either their hearing of God's message or properly responding to it.

Do we have that same problem today? Yes. Our discernment can become clouded in the same way the Israelites' discernment became clouded, and for some of the same reasons.

THE CARES OF LIFE

The cares of life can prevent us from hearing what God is saying to us. Jesus taught that the seed of the message about His kingdom could be choked out by thorns, "'the worries of this life and the deceitfulness of wealth'" (Matthew 13:22).

The demands and problems of life can not only choke out new seed, but they can also prevent us from receiving God's answer. We can become so caught up in handling our own needs and troubles that we are robbed of effective ministries.

We are just barely able to survive ourselves and can hardly think about helping someone else.

Before the deliverance from Egypt, the Israelites suffered in a very oppressive situation. The circumstances made it difficult for them to hear Moses initially when he came to deliver them from slavery. "The Israelites . . . did not listen to him because of their discouragement and cruel bondage" (Exodus 6:9).

Often the secret to our own need being met is found when we reach out in ministry to others. "The Lord turned the captivity of Job, when he prayed for his friends" (Job 42:10, KJV).

SELECTIVE HEARING

Have you ever been part of a group where several people were talking to each other at the same time? You tuned out all of the voices except those you wanted to hear. That's an example of selective hearing. If you listened to a tape recording of that same group conversation, you would notice that it was just an indistinguishable jumble of people's voices. They were all recorded at the same intensity. Unlike your selective hearing which sorted out the sounds and voices, the recorder picked up every voice equally. Selective listening, or hearing only what we want to hear and tuning out the rest, interferes with hearing all that God would speak to us. Jesus indicated that it is a choice we make to obey or to shut our ears to the things God desires to speak to us. "'He who has ears, let him hear'" (Matthew 11:15).

PRECONCEIVED IDEAS

Preconceived ideas can keep us from understanding what God is saying to us. The Jewish people, for the most part, did not recognize Jesus as the Messiah because they were expecting an earthly king.

Even the Spirit-filled New Testament church had its share of difficulty in comprehending what God was doing. Again, because of preconceived ideas, they did not understand they were to reach out to the Gentiles. God had planned all along to include the Gentiles. Israel had been established as a nation with that end in mind. God's express word to Abraham at the founding of the nation of Israel was, "'All peoples on earth will be blessed through you'" (Genesis 12:3).

COMFORT ZONES

We tend to like comfortable situations. However, in order to be in a position to hear God's voice and then respond, we must break out of our comfortable and sometimes rigid thinking patterns and ways of doing things. We need to fight the tendency to be locked in to doing things only one way. "Congealed thinking is the forerunner of failure . . . make sure you are always receptive to new ideas."[1]

God's Voice to the World

How does God speak to the world? Through several sources. Romans 1 tells us that creation speaks to the human heart about God's existence: "What may be known about God is plain to them, because God has made it plain to them. For since the creation of the world God's invisible qualities—his eternal power and divine nature—have been clearly seen, being understood from what has been made, so that men are without excuse" (1:19,20).

And as John 6:44 says, the Holy Spirit speaks to the hearts of people, drawing them into a relationship with God.

The world generally does not read the Bible or spend a great deal of time in prayer. However, Romans 10:14 asks the question, "How can they believe in the one of whom they have not heard?"

Believers, as representatives of Christ, are the only Bible many people in the world read. Paul reminds the believers at Corinth of this: "You yourselves are our letter, written on our hearts, known and read by everybody. You show that you are a letter from Christ ... written not with ink but with the Spirit of the living God, not on tablets of stone but on tablets of human hearts" (2 Corinthians 3:2,3).

Understanding how God speaks to the world, answer these questions from your perspective:

- How are we, as the Church, doing in our task of speaking to the world?
- How is God speaking to the world through you?

A George Barna survey of non-Christians indicates that the communication of the gospel fails to influence the world for three major reasons:

- Unbelievers do not understand how Christianity relates to their lives.
- Unbelievers do not understand what Christians are trying to say. Christians tend to have their own jargon, which is unfamiliar to the world.
- Unbelievers are more concerned with what is currently happening in their lives than they are with eternity. The solution of Christ's death and resurrection is not the kind of solution they are looking for to solve their problems.[2]

These survey results make it apparent that we need to make some changes if we are to effectively communicate the gospel to our culture.

When the church is truly alive, it brings life to a dying world. When unbelievers find Christ, the world is a better place and the church is healthy. But the church cannot be healthy without a focus on the harvest. A church that becomes only a storage area for that which is already harvested will soon find itself depleted. A church that is not involved in some part of the harvest process is dying.

Revival is occurring in some places, and scores of unbelievers are being brought into the kingdom of God. Where revival is not happening, the burden is on the church to find ways to move outside the walls of its building and go out to touch the world.

God's Voice for These Times

God desires to speak to us individually, and to the church collectively, that we may in turn speak to the world. How are we responding? What is He saying to us about our lives?

In 1 Chronicles we find the story of a traumatic time for the Jewish people. Saul, Israel's first king, had been killed in battle. David, who had been anointed years earlier by Samuel, was now king. The various leaders of the tribes of Israel came to David at Hebron to transfer their allegiance to David. Tucked in the midst of this long list of tribes and numbers is this line about the "men of Issachar, who understood the times and knew what Israel should do" (1 Chronicles 12:32).

Think for a moment. What if every church understood the times and knew what to do? What if all the classes and ministries in each local church were led by individuals who understood the times and knew what to do?

- Believers would understand how to properly relate to the group of people they were called to minister to.
- Believers would understand the situations that individuals in their particular area of ministry were struggling with.
- Believers would know the right words to speak to encourage them.
- Believers would understand the keys to touch the heart of each child, teen, or adult in their class.
- Believers would know the best way to reach the lost in their neighborhood or city.

The exciting part is that God desires to speak to us about the times we live in and what we should do. He desires for us to be avenues of His voice to a hurting world. Think about these questions as you think about being God's representative to a world that doesn't know Him.

- In what terms do you think God would like to speak to the world?
- What are the terms people would understand?

- Are you currently speaking in terms they can understand?
- What could you say or do that would open people's hearts?
- In what areas would people allow you to touch their lives?

What time is it? God wants us to know. There are three ways we can get insight into the times we are living in:

- We must understand what the Scriptures tell us about our times.
- We must use our natural senses to observe what is happening in the world around us.
- Most important, we must listen to what the voice of God would speak to our hearts.

UNDERSTANDING THE SCRIPTURES

The Bible tells us much about our times: "There will be terrible times in the last days" (2 Timothy 3:1); "Do this [love one another], understanding the present time. The hour has come for you to wake up from your slumber, because our salvation is nearer now than when we first believed" (Romans 13:11). We know that it is still day—working time—but the "night is coming, when no one can work" (John 9:4). "It is time to seek the Lord, until he comes and showers righteousness on you" (Hosea 10:12).

We know the truths of the Bible intellectually, but we have heard them so many times that it has been easy to become callous to them. Read the Bible with a sensitivity to the Spirit, allowing Him to give you an urgency of these times and the need to reach out to the world with a message of hope.

USING YOUR NATURAL SENSES

We must be aware of what is happening around us. Everything that we see, hear, and feel gives us information about our world. A vast amount of information is available about the times in which we live.

We are living in the Information Age. More information is

available concerning current issues than any one individual could process. Availing ourselves of some of the applicable material should enable us to draw some conclusions about our times.

It has been said "Information is power." This truth is backed up by Scripture. Hosea states, "'My people are destroyed from lack of knowledge'" (Hosea 4:6). They purposely rejected the truth available to them through the prophets and God's Word. They were being destroyed by the world's sinful ways because they chose not to know His Word and through it to know Him. They had the power to live for God available to them through His Word, but their rejection of it left them ignorant and powerless to do right.

People look at the sky and can tell by the clouds that it will rain. Or if the sky is red in the evening, we know the next day will be nice. We know because we've seen the signs and the events before. Jesus rebuked the people of His day. "'You know how to interpret the appearance of the sky, but you cannot interpret the signs of the times'" (Matthew 16:3). The religious leaders could read the signs in the sky, but they failed to recognize the signs of the times that would tell them the Messiah they had been waiting for had come.

There are signs available to us too, if we are willing to read them. Statistics and surveys are taken daily, telling us what the American people are feeling and thinking on every issue imaginable. Statistics give us information on topics such as how big our task is, the percentage of Americans currently attending church, the people groups that are largely ignored by the church, and age groups that are most likely to embrace the gospel.

Surveys are fascinating tools that, if used properly, can make us more effective in the harvest field. By tracking statistics for several years, trends can be predicted based on what has happened in the past. They can show us what we as a nation are thinking and can give us direction as to areas of need. Religious polls give us insight into church attitudes and actions.

They point out areas that are deteriorating and need attention and offer clues as to how we can become more effective.

One danger needs to be noted at this point. Polls should not set our moral or our spiritual compass as a church. It is possible to misuse polls and allow them to alter our message, rather than using them as a tool to show where we are and to determine if our methods are working. Although we must remain open to new methods, we are not open to a new message.

George Barna says, "Ultimately, statistics are meaningless. The decision to accept or reject Christ is between the person and God, regardless of the laws of averages. The averages, however, are based on patterns of behavior that might help us know how to be more sensitive to people's openness and needs."[3]

Statistics tell only part of the story. They do not tell us everything that will happen in the future. How many times have you heard the comment "Who could have predicted this?" Sometimes God may desire us to do something contrary to established wisdom.

LISTENING TO GOD'S VOICE

God desires us to know not only what time it is, but also what we should do. How can we know what we ought to do? There is no formula or shortcut. We must hear from God. We should avail ourselves of the latest technology, tools, and ideas. However, God must put something within our hearts for our particular situation because every place and every individual is different. We would do well to heed Solomon's advice, "'Get wisdom, get understanding; do not forget my words or swerve from them. . . . Wisdom is supreme; therefore get wisdom. Though it cost all you have, get understanding'" (Proverbs 4:5,7).

There are things on the horizon that the Spirit of God would like us to be ahead of, rather than behind. His Spirit would like to speak direction to our hearts for these times.

Some of that direction may come as a word of warning. "By faith, Noah, when warned about things not yet seen, in holy fear, built an ark to save his family" (Hebrews 11:7). Noah's sensitivity to the word God spoke to him and his obedience to that word resulted in the saving of his family.

Some of the direction God would like to give us may involve new areas or ways of ministry that we may be overlooking. Peter heard from God concerning ministering to Cornelius. As a result, the door was opened to a group of people whom the New Testament church had been blind to ministering to, the Gentiles (Acts 10).

Ananias was told by the Lord, "'Go to the house of Judas on Straight Street and ask for a man from Tarsus named Saul, for he is praying. In a vision he has seen a man named Ananias come and place his hands on him to restore his sight'" (Acts 9:11,12). The Early Church may not have had an idea that Saul was a prospect for Christianity.

It is interesting to note that in the cases of both Saul and Cornelius, God prepared their hearts in advance to receive the message. God has people, many of them already prepared by the work of others, whom He would like to bring into our lives so we may affect them in some positive way in the harvest process.

Getting Ready to Go Out

We must find the way to motivate the church to action. We must find the way to present the gospel so that many in the world will respond to it. If people are approached in the right way at the right time, and with patience, many will respond.

When Jesus said, "Go," He had something in mind that would work for this generation. God, who knows all hearts and knows all communities, also knows the keys that will open the doors to those hearts and communities.

We need to take time to hear God's voice. When our hearts cry out for the lost in our families and neighborhoods and we seek God's face for them, God will show us ways to reach them. Some of the direction God would like to give us may concern how to best deal with the people in our lives whom we already love and care about.

We need to learn to discern God's voice in the midst of all the other voices that would confuse us and throw us off track. Discernment is one of the most-needed attributes in the church today. We need to be open, but this does not mean gullible. "Do not believe every spirit, but test the spirits to see whether they are from God, because many false prophets have gone out into the world" (1 John 4:1).

Every trend that occurs in the church world is not always the will of God. We need a sensitive spirit in tune with God's times and seasons. We need to learn to cooperate with God in purposeful outreach to those who need His love in their lives.

Being Open to Change

We must be willing to make the necessary changes in our personal lives, ministries, and church.

Change is often uncomfortable. Try the following exercise. Clasp your hands together in a comfortable manner with the fingers of one hand laced through the fingers of the other hand. Hold them like that for a few seconds. Now, simply switch each finger one over and clasp again. Hold this position for a few seconds. Notice how uncomfortable it is. You want to move back to the familiar and comfortable position you are used to.

There may be comfortable areas of our lives and thinking that if simply adjusted a little would make us more effective. Occasionally, we all need heart and attitude tune-ups.

History tells us that change is often resisted by the church. When John Wycliffe translated the Bible into English in the 14th century, he was excommunicated. A small elite group "did not like his idea of enabling the common man to read and understand God's Word. Had he not died of natural causes, he might have suffered the same fate as many of his followers, being burned at the stake. As it was, Wycliffe's enemies hated what he had done so much that 40 years later they dug up his bones and threw them into a stream."[4]

William Tyndale printed the first English Bible in the 16th century. For his efforts to make God's Word more accessible to the people, "Tyndale was bound to a stake, strangled and cremated."[5]

While we may not respond to change in such a drastic manner, we probably would agree with Mark Twain, "The only person who likes change is a wet baby."[6]

Some changes are good; some changes are bad. We should not change just for the sake of change. We need wisdom in deciding what changes to make in our lives and ministries. It may help to ask ourselves the following questions:

- If we continue in the way we are headed in our ministry, where will we end up?
- Does God want to put something new in our hearts and do something new in our lives?
- Are we willing to make the changes necessary, even if they infringe on our personal likes and dislikes or our time?

What does Scripture say about the new things that God would like to do? "'Forget the former things; do not dwell on the past. See, I am doing a new thing! Now it springs up; do you not perceive it? I am making a way in the desert and streams in the wasteland'" (Isaiah 43:18,19).

When we hear the phrase "new thing," it may trigger a selfish response in us. We tend to get excited, thinking that this verse means some new spiritual thrill or way of getting Holy Ghost goose bumps. Too often, this interpretation is the main focus of "new things" for the church—something for us. This type of thinking results in a church that stays within its walls, affecting no one. This is in direct opposition to a harvest mentality that always keeps a focus on the lost. A harvest mentality will result in the real spiritual thrills we long for as we see people in whom we have invested coming into the kingdom of God.

We love the former things. There is nothing inherently wrong with the former things. They have made us what we are today. But we cannot live on yesterday's experiences. We must build on and learn from the past. Yesterday's methods may or may not be the way God will do things today and tomorrow.

Developing Ministries That Meet Needs

Every church and community has areas of ministry that still need to be developed. We may have written off people around us as too difficult to reach. God can make ways in the desert and create streams in the wastelands of our cities.

"'The former things have taken place, and new things I declare; before they spring into being I announce them to you'" (Isaiah 42:9). There are things God would like to whisper into our hearts before they even happen. He would like to orchestrate our lives so that we show up at people's points of need. He would like to move us so that we are ahead of situations in our families instead of picking up the broken pieces afterwards.

God would like to birth vision in our hearts for new ministries that have not yet started and new ways of revitalizing current ministries. He can give us insight into ministries to be developed now for future needs. "'I will tell you of new things, of hidden things unknown to you. They are created now, and not long ago; you have not heard of them before today. So you cannot say, "Yes, I knew of them"'" (Isaiah 48:6,7).

This verse should excite us and shake us up. God would like to show us hidden things that we do not know. He has ways of doing things that He has not yet revealed to us, even in our thoughts.

Keeping the Enemy in Perspective

Great sports rivalries generally produce great games, but not high-scoring games. The score is frequently very close because the two teams play each other so often that they know how to defend against each other.

The enemy will try to stop every work of God, but he is not omniscient. Satan does not have a defense for the thought God has not yet given. This is illustrated often in Scripture. Herod thought he had the perfect plan to destroy the infant Jesus. He would kill all the males under two years of age in Bethlehem. However, an angel of the Lord appeared to Joseph in a dream. "Get up," he said, "take the child and his mother and escape to Egypt" (Matthew 2).

God, the source of all wisdom and knowledge, has promised to give us the resources we need for our lives and ministries if we ask. "If any of you lacks wisdom, he should ask God, who gives generously to all without finding fault, and it will be given to him" (James 1:5).

Endnotes

[1] John C. Maxwell, *Leadership 101* (Tulsa: Honor Books, 1995), 70.

[2] George Barna, *Evangelism That Works* (Ventura, Calif.: Regal Books, 1995), 40.

[3] Ibid., 112.

[4] Francis Anfuso, *Jesus Ain't Plain Vanilla,* video presentation, 21st Century Ministries, 1993.

[5] Ibid.

[6] Quoted in "What Is Vision, Anyway?" *Leadership Magazine,* Summer 1994, 25.

4
Love in Action

Have you ever had the experience of going into a church filled with only elderly people? As wonderful as those people may be, you quickly realize that unless young couples and children are brought into the church, eventually it will be forced to close its doors. The church is only a generation away from extinction if the old die and there are no young to replace them.

The "Just for Us" Philosophy

During the 1960s and 1970s a generation called the "baby boomers" rebelled against organized religion, and many left their churches. Their return to church in the mid-1980s was precipitated by the birth of their children and a desire to fill the religious void in their lives. However, baby boomers once again began leaving the churches in the 1990s.

According to George Barna, 85 percent of all nonchurched adults have had a prolonged period of time during which they consistently attended a church or religious center. Barna observed, "For people to leave, they often must be driven away. The dechurched admitted that if the church they had been attending had understood them and ministered to them effectively, they would have stayed."[1]

This trend of exiting the church affects us a great deal. That this exodus can happen without our even being aware of it is alarming. We can become so caught up in our own lives, enjoying our church friends and activities, that people can enter our churches, stay awhile, and leave without our realizing it. We notice their departure only if it happens to affect our family or our sphere of close relationships.

Once or twice while pastoring, someone asked, "Pastor, when are we going to have a service just for us?" My answer was, "When there is just us here." A "just for us" focus will eventually result in "just us" being here. We always have a responsibility to the unconverted who may be in our midst.

This "just for us" philosophy reveals itself in our attitudes and actions. This is not a new problem. In Luke 19 we are told of a man named Zacchaeus who worked for the IRS of his day. Although as a tax collector he had gained wealth, Zacchaeus was evidently seeking for something that was missing in his life.

Jesus was passing through the city of Jericho, where Zaccaeus lived. Zacchaeus had probably heard about Jesus and wanted to see who He was. Because of his short stature and the large crowd, Zacchaeus found a high vantage point that enabled him to see over the crowd. He may have been like those who crowd the overpasses of our highways hoping for a glimpse of a celebrity when one is known to be passing through.

Zacchaeus' vantage point happened to be a tree. When Jesus passed by, He noticed Zacchaeus, invited him down, and told him He would be coming to his home that day. What a thrill for Zacchaeus!

However, the religious people of that day did not like Jesus being a guest at the home of a sinner. But Jesus left all of them and went with the man who needed Him. Jesus had to remind them that "'the Son of Man came to seek and to save what was lost'" (Luke 19:10).

Family Members or Guests?

At times some in the church may resent any attention given to the guest rather than to them. Some may have the attitude of the board member who said, "Pastor, you didn't shake my hand last Sunday." The pastor had walked by the board member to shake the hand of a visitor.

"I'm sorry, I thought you were family," the pastor said.

Family members know where the towels are, where the refrigerator is, and where the thermostat is. They feel free to use those items as needed. However, when overnight guests visit the home, the whole family becomes involved in making the guests' stay as pleasant as possible. They put clean sheets on the bed and put out the guest towels. A few extra touches are added to the meal that is to be served. When the guests awake in the morning, they are asked how they slept and if they were too hot or too cold.

The visitor at church deserves to receive equal attention. "Family" members should do everything they can to make that visit enjoyable. Rick Warren, author of *The Purpose Driven Church,* suggests thinking of visitors as guests because "the term 'visitor' implies they're not here to stay and the term 'guest' implies that this is someone for whom you do everything you can to make the person feel comfortable."[2]

When this topic of attending to guests is mentioned, many people react by saying, "We don't need to change anything; we don't want to compromise the message." Giving proper attention to guests is not changing the message. It is just doing what we can to make sure the message we want to communicate is received and understood. People receive a message that starts before they even get in the door. We want to do what we can to make sure they are hearing the right message.

Our city's hospital had a chemical dependency unit with a 30-day treatment program. Once checked into that program, the patients were not allowed to leave the hospital except to attend Sunday services at the church of their choice. Because we were the only church in that community running a van to and from the hospital on Sunday mornings, many of the individuals in that program chose to visit us. Many of them had no church background and came from very difficult and ungodly lifestyles.

It was our privilege to minister to many of those alcoholics, a number of whom eventually made decisions for Christ and became part of our church. For a while, because of a lack of space in our building, this group met during the Sunday school hour in a trailer located on the church property, then walked to the church for morning worship.

Many of those people also had a smoking habit. To the dismay of some of the saints, they would use the time between Sunday school and church to have a cigarette. One of the ushers observed this and came into my office just prior to the morning worship service and said, "Pastor, now they're smoking on the front steps of the church. What are we going to do?"

"Don't chase them away!" I replied. "Leave them alone! I haven't even had the opportunity to preach to them yet. If they never come back, we can't reach them."

First Impressions

At a special event where the church was packed and chairs had been placed in the aisles, along the back, and in the foyer, I was happy to see the parking lot was also jammed. People were parking their cars at the neighboring gas station and walking over to the church. An usher, also looking out the window, exclaimed, "Oh, no! More people! Now what are we going to do?"

Although the usher's response came from the frustration of wondering where more chairs could be placed, too often that is the message the visitor receives by our actions.

Sometimes before individuals even come in the front door of a church, they receive the message that they are not welcome. Visitors form an opinion about your church within the first 10 minutes of their arrival. They decide whether or not to come back long before the pastor speaks. First impressions do count. Rick Warren said, "The way many churches welcome visitors causes them to experience their three greatest fears all at once!" Visitors are asked to "Please stand up; tell us your name and a little about yourself."[3]

We must occasionally look at our ministries through the eyes of the first-time visitor. We want visitors to come back. We are trying to reach them. The purpose in evaluating the message our church may be sending does not involve compromising our message; instead, it is becoming aware of things we might be doing that would keep our message from being properly received.

Insiders and Outsiders

There are often two different worlds in a church. Those who are seeking and worshiping God fill the front half of the church. The visitor and the unconverted are most likely to sit in the back.

Rick Warren suggests you view the visitor in two categories: "Insiders" are those who come from backgrounds similar to ours and understand everything that is happening, and "outsiders" are those who don't have a clue what is going on. We need to remember that not everything we do is familiar to nonbelievers. They do not automatically know where to go, where to turn to in their Bibles, or where the songbooks are.

We will not keep everyone who visits, for not everyone will like our style and message. However, if we consistently lose everyone in the back of the church, something needs to change. The message needs to penetrate beyond the front half of a church or class.

Sometimes people who are seeking God come into our churches and look in on our lives. By our words and actions, we can let them walk away or even drive them away. Most of the time this is done in ignorance; we are not aware they are even there. It is possible to unintentionally drive away the lost or the new convert. If we do not know they left, we're not concerned about where they went or why they left.

It takes continual effort to keep from losing those who visit, for the church easily focuses on the adult flock already in the fold. Without intending to do so, our attention automatically shifts to a maintenance mode. We find ourselves concentrating on not losing those we already have.

Our idea of church growth can deteriorate to concentrating on transfer growth from other churches. If we are in an area that supports more than one church in our fellowship, we may even get a little excited if another church nearby is having difficulty. We hope that some of their people might come our direction.

The church needs to ask itself this sobering question: Does it hurt more when a tithe payer walks away and says, "I'll never come back to this church," or when a sinner walks away and says, "If that is what Christianity is all about, I want no part of it"? The tithe payer will probably just go to another church. The chances are that, unless someone intervenes, the sinner will not try church again. We must be aware of the message we are sending so that outsiders are not turned away from the church and lost.

Caring for Spiritual Children

Abortion is horrible. It is a blight on our nation. But what is more amazing is that Christians who will stand in picket lines at an abortion clinic do not blink an eye at the spiritual abortion that occurs every day. We never see a protest against spiritual abortion.

Listen to God's rebuke to the shepherds of Israel. "'You have not brought back the strays or searched for the lost. . . . My sheep . . . were scattered over the whole earth, and no one searched or looked for them'" (Ezekiel 34:4–6).

Every church should consider the following questions:

- Who is watching out for the spiritual children?
- Who is caring for the spiritually unborn in our community?
- Who is in charge of the spiritual prenatal care for the church?
- Who is in charge of the spiritual nursery?

Jacob is an example of one who cared for the young. The meeting of Jacob and Esau after years of estrangement is found in Genesis 33. Jacob had run away 20 years before because Esau threatened to kill him after Jacob cheated him out of his birthright. Jacob was apprehensive about returning home with his family and flocks when he learned Esau was coming to meet him. But verse 4 tells us, "Esau ran to meet Jacob and embraced him; he threw his arms around his neck and kissed him. And they wept."

When Esau suggested that they make the rest of the journey home together, Jacob said to him, "'My lord knows that the children are tender and that I must care for the ewes and cows that are nursing their young. If they are driven hard just one day, all the animals will die. So let my lord go on ahead of his servant, while I move along slowly at the pace of the droves before me and that of the children'" (Genesis 33:12–14).

Jacob's concern according to these verses was that the children and the flocks with young might survive the journey. Jacob's children were important to him. His sons ensured that his family line would continue. He also realized that if the newborn animals and those with child died, he would have no future financially.

Jacob was a shepherd. He knew these concerns were important. Our Good Shepherd also cares personally for the young. Isaiah speaks of God's comfort for His lambs. "He tends his flock like a shepherd: He gathers the lambs in his arms and carries them close to his heart; he gently leads those that have young" (Isaiah 40:11).

In speaking to the church in Thessalonica, Paul reminded

them of how he had treated them. "We were gentle among you, like a mother caring for her little children. We loved you so much that we were delighted to share with you not only the gospel of God but our lives as well, because you had become so dear to us" (1 Thessalonians 2:7,8). Every Christian needs to feel this way about the spiritually unborn and newborn.

Idle Christians are like idle hands—open to mischief. A church is healthy when souls are being saved and church members are busy taking care of the newborn Christians. Being involved with caring for all the needs of a newborn keeps Christians too busy to be bothered with little grievances. When we are concerned about our sons or daughters or our friends being nurtured by the church family, we pitch in and help to assure that they survive the journey.

Babies are a lot of work. Their total dependence on us complicates our schedules and takes a lot of our time, and they require a great deal of care. But they are also wonderful gifts. They bring joy into our lives and take our minds off ourselves. We are forced to focus on their needs. Parents who have to get up in the middle of the night to feed a baby feel like turning over and going back to sleep, but because they love that baby and want that baby to grow and be happy, they get up and care for it. Good parents put their child's needs above their own desires.

If souls are being saved in our church, we become spiritual parents or caretakers. We may fail to be the nurturing parents to these spiritually dependent newborns that we should be. Many factors can keep us from properly caring for the spiritually unborn and newborn among us.

Obstacles to Nurturing

Lack of Focus

We may fail to see the need to nurture. Young pastors who are beginning a pioneer work or who are going into small churches desire to break through walls of resistance and touch their communities. More experienced pastors with larger congregations also want to be effective shepherds of their flocks. I advise them to "keep a 20/20/20 vision."

We know that 20/20 vision is perfect vision—no glasses needed. What is 20/20/20 vision? It's good spiritual vision, or a harvest mentality. Though pastors have numerous other obligations and duties, they should keep their ministries on course by focusing firmly on the harvest.

I suggest that they spend 20 hours a week in prayer, preparation, and presentation; 20 hours a week in the normal day-to-day administrative details of running a church (such things as visitation and committee meetings); and 20 hours focusing on lost people or ministry to them. That is often the hard part, but it can be as simple as associating with lost people, sitting with them at community events, having coffee with them, getting to know them, and developing friendships.

All Christians should focus a percentage of their discretionary time on developing relationships with the lost. This is part of working in the harvest. We must know people if we want to be aware of their needs and be a spiritual nurturer.

BUSYNESS

We have many demands on our time. Our church schedule can become so busy and take so much energy that we have no time to spend with lost people. We find it difficult to think of adding one more thing to our lives.

Charles H. Spurgeon made this suggestion regarding the use of our time:

> Select a large box, and place in it as many cannon balls as it will hold, and it is, after a fashion, full; but it will hold more if smaller matters be found. Bring a quantity of marbles; very many of these may be packed in the spaces between the larger globes; the box is now full, but still only in a sense; it will contain more yet. There are spaces in abundance, into which you

may shake a considerable quantity of small shot, and the chest is now filled beyond all question; but yet there is room. You cannot put in another shot of marble, much less another ball; but you will find that several pounds of sand will slide down between the larger materials, and, even then between the granules of sand, if you empty yonder jug, there will be space for all the water, and for the same quantity several times repeated. Where there is no space for the great, there may be room for the little; where the little cannot enter, the less can make its way; and where the less is shut out, the least of all may find ample room. So where time is, as we say, fully occupied, there must be stray moments, occasional intervals, and bits of time which might hold a vast amount of usefulness in the course of months and years.[4]

Here is one of the applications we can make from this illustration: Learn to prioritize. Because of the busyness of our lives, we must take care of the weightier matters of life first. We often reverse the process and allow the trivial, or even the urgent, to crowd out the important.

Attending a funeral has a way of restoring a proper perspective to life. Every time we stand at a casket, we are reminded of our own and of others' mortality. Unimportant things that consume so much of our time and thinking are suddenly pushed into the background as we are faced with the only thing that is really important—where people will spend eternity.

ISOLATION

People who come to Christ for salvation often bring with them some of their unsaved friends and relatives who have seen the change in their lives. They are excited about what God has done for them, and they want other sinners to experience what they did. However, after a period of time, an isolation factor seems to set in, because the only people they know on an impact (friend) level and socialize with are other believers. Isolation from the spiritually unborn will prevent us from ever nurturing them into a new life.

George Barna suggests that it would be interesting for church people to write down the names of their close unsaved friends. "You might be surprised at how few names would appear on those lists. Yet, it is that group of nonbelievers we are called to reach through the creditability of an authentic, caring friendship."[5]

Discomfort

Imagine this scenario: You are part of a group of 50 Christians at a social event in a huge hall. In that hall are also 450 nonbelievers. The Christians are given the assignment to mingle and become friends with nonbelievers during the next three hours. After a half hour or so, you would probably notice that several of the Christians have quit mingling and are gathered together in a corner visiting with each other. An hour or so later, more of the initial group of 50 are gathered together. At the close of three hours, probably only one or two Christians are carrying out their assignment.

This grouping together of Christians would happen for several reasons. We are more comfortable with people we know, with those who are like us, and with those who hold the same values we do. We enjoy being with people who know us and accept us. It takes effort to move outside our comfort zone, where people may initially give us a cold shoulder and may not understand how we live and view life.

However, if we are to touch this world, if we are to know those who are lost, if we are to nurture the spiritually unborn, then we must risk moving into some of those uncomfortable situations.

Overwhelming Need

This world's needs are great. The magnitude of the need can boggle our minds. It is beyond our abilities to even think about having any effect on it. So, because we cannot change the world and minister to all the needs, we may be tempted to do nothing.

As a man was walking along the beach, he noticed that thousands of starfish had washed up and been left on the shore when the tide went out. Realizing the fish would die if their surroundings did not change quickly, the man reached down and began throwing them back into the water one by one.

Another man stopped to watch. After seeing the first man throw several of the fish back into the sea, he asked, "Why bother? There is no way you will be able to throw all these fish back before they die."

The first man replied, "No, but it will sure mean a lot to this fish."

We may not be able to reach everyone, but it will mean a lot to the ones we do reach. We must focus on the individual's need so that we're not overwhelmed by the magnitude of the needs of the many.

CONFRONTATIONAL WITNESSING PROGRAMS

Another barrier to involving ourselves with the unsaved is the pressure that has been put on us by the church to become involved in confrontational witnessing programs. We feel the pressure to do it all today or we feel we have failed. We are wise enough to realize that this approach may not work too well with our neighbors and friends. We often feel so guilty that we do not do the things we know they would respond to.

As Pentecostals who believe in the working and leading of the Holy Spirit, we should have an increased sensitivity to the unsaved. Few people respond well to being confronted and told they need to be saved. The most effective witnessing occurs when we are able to communicate with people. We can ask them about the things that interest them—their families, their hobbies, their work. As we listen closely, we will often pick up on something that bothers them or some problem they have. That's when we can guide the conversation toward spiritual things and the One who can help them. We may be able to pray with them, or to tell them we will pray for the problem they have (and mean it), or to actually lead them to salvation. Witnessing can occur daily without being confrontational to the unsaved and scary to us.

IMPATIENCE

We live in a society that is built on instant gratification. We want it all and we want it all right now. We like to do a project quickly, then settle back in our easy chairs. However, evangelism is a process that requires patience. Taking Christ to people requires time and effort. Talking about reaching the lost is easier than actually doing it.

In *The Brothers Karamazov,* the Russian novelist Fyodor Dostoyevsky reveals a character that may seem familiar.

> I love mankind . . . but I am amazed at myself: the more I love mankind in general, the less I love people in particular, that is, individually, as separate persons. In my dreams . . . I often went so far as to think passionately of serving mankind, and, it may be, would really have gone to the cross for people if it were somehow suddenly necessary, and yet I am incapable of living in the same room with anyone for even two days, this I know from experience. As soon as someone is there, close to me, his personality oppresses my self-esteem and restricts my freedom. In twenty-four hours I can to hate even the best of men: one because he takes too long eating his dinner, another because he has a cold and keeps blowing his nose. . . . On the other hand, it has always happened that the more I hate people individually, the more ardent becomes my love for humanity as a whole.[6]

We may not express it in the same terms, but that man's thinking probably strikes a chord in all of us. In this busy world, we too speak often of our love for the lost. We can imagine great exploits and talk about our love for the lost, but true love is an action. When God's love is shed abroad in our hearts by the Holy Spirit, we go beyond imagining what we could do—we get involved in doing it. We involve ourselves in individual lives and needs of the lost and invest time in them. We move out of our isolation and comfort. We care for the young and nurture the newborn and the spiritually unborn. We are gentle, like a mother caring for her little children, because love is an action. Involvement in people's lives is what will open the doors to their hearts.

Endnotes

[1] George Barna, *Evangelism That Works* (Ventura, Calif.: Regal Books, 1995), 50.

[2] Rick Warren, *The Purpose Driven Church* (Grand Rapids: Zondervan Publishing House, 1995), 260, 261.

[3] Ibid., 257, 260.

[4] Charles H. Spurgeon, quoted in Pam Young and Peggy Jones, *Sidetracked Home Executives* (New York: Warner Books, Inc., 1981), 40.

[5] Barna, *Evangelism That Works,* 130.

[6] Fyodor Dostoyevsky (translated from the Russian by Richard Pevear and Larissa Volokchonsky), *The Brothers Karamazov* (New York: Alfred A. Knopf, Inc., 1990), 57.

5
Finding the Key

In 2 Samuel 14 we read of the woman who came to David to appeal to him to bring back his son, Absalom, who had been banished from him for three years. In reasoning with David, she spoke a truth that struck a chord in David's heart. "'God . . . devises ways so a banished person may not be estranged from him'" (2 Samuel 14:14). This verse tells us that God looks for and makes ways for those who are lost to return to Him. That is our task also. We must look for keys to reach the hearts of lost people and bring them to Christ.

Perching on the Precipice

A pastor friend tells this story from his childhood. At 12 years of age, he was left to care for his 2-year-old brother for a couple of hours while his parents were gone. Thinking his brother was sleeping, he went outside for a few moments. Hearing a noise above him, he glanced up at the roof and saw to his horror that his little brother had crawled out a dormer window onto the roof and was perched on the edge of the roof pretending to be Superman, his hero, saying "I can fly! I can fly!"

The older brother said, "I looked up and knew that I had to do something quickly. I also realized that if I did the wrong thing, he might jump and be seriously injured or perhaps even killed." Not wanting to startle his little brother, he grabbed a ladder and climbed quickly and quietly up to an opposite edge of the roof, resisting the urge to yell or scream for fear the boy might jump. "I thought I had my best chance of saving him by trying to make him want to come to me," this pastor said.

"That experience shaped my whole ministry philosophy. My goal now is to keep men and women from jumping off the ledge into an eternity without the Lord. I do it by helping them want to come to Christ."

We are ministering to a world perched on a precipice. Like that child, nonbelievers are not aware of how precarious their position is. Our job is to try to keep them from going over that precipice to certain destruction. We can do things that will make them run from us and jump off the ledge or we can do things that will make them want to come to Jesus. Our task is to do whatever it takes to save as many as possible.

Identifying With the Lost

Paul told us his secret of influencing people for Christ:

> I have freely and happily become a servant of any and all so that I can win them to Christ. When I am with the Jews I seem as one of them so that they will listen to the Gospel and I can win them to Christ. When I am with the Gentiles who follow Jewish customs and ceremonies I don't argue, even though I don't agree, because I want to help them. When with the heathen I agree with them as much as I can, except of course that I must always do what is right as a Christian. And so, by agreeing, I can win their confidence and help them too.
>
> When I am with those whose conscience bothers them easily, I don't act as though I know it all and don't say they are foolish; the result is that they are willing to let me help them. Yes,

whatever a person is like, I try to find common ground with him so that he will let me tell him about Christ and let Christ save him. I do this to get the Gospel to them and also for the blessing I myself receive when I see them come to Christ (1 Corinthians 9:19–23, *The Living Bible*).

Rick Warren, in his book *The Purpose Driven Church,* tells what a great fisherman his father is. "Ten of us could be fishing the same lake and my dad would catch all the fish. . . .

"As I got older, I realized his secret: My dad understood fish. He could 'read' a lake and figure out exactly where the fish were: he knew what time of day they liked to eat; he knew what bait or lure to use depending on the type of fish; he knew when to change bait as the temperature changed; he even seemed to know exactly how deep to drop the line into the water. He made it as easy and attractive as possible for fish to swallow his hook—so they did! He caught fish on their terms."[1]

Jude also recognized that you deal with different people in different ways: "Be merciful to those who doubt; snatch others from the fire and save them; to others show mercy, mixed with fear—hating even the clothing stained by corrupted flesh" (Jude 22,23).

There is an appropriate time and place for dealing with people, and various ways of doing so. People are more receptive at some times more than others, and to certain ideas more than others. Rick Warren states, "Spiritual receptivity is something that comes and goes in people's lives like an ocean tide. At various times in life people tend to be more open to spiritual truth than at other times. God uses a variety of tools to soften hearts and prepare people to be saved."[2]

Whether we are breaking hard ground or the shoots are springing quickly through the fertile soil, we must carefully tend the seeds that take root. With all types of people—those who are hard-hearted, those ignorant about God, those too busy to serve Him, or those who are spiritually hungry—we need to look for the keys that will open hearts and lives to the gospel. These keys are most often in the preparation, planting, or nurturing stage of the harvest process.

Some Christians feel that their responsibility is only to deliver the message and that it is the other people's problem if they do not respond. That is only partially correct, for we are responsible for presenting our message in a way that people can understand and process. The ability to communicate a message depends on having someone who will listen.

The old adage "You can lead a horse to water, but you cannot make him drink" is true. As much as we may want to, we cannot force people to respond. However, when dealing with the people we love and are concerned about, we want to do more than lead them to water; we would like to see them drink.

This desire needs to extend beyond our immediate family and circle of friends. Jesus was "not wanting anyone to perish, but everyone to come to repentance" (2 Peter 3:9). People who don't know Jesus are sitting on the precipice. We want them to come to safety, but we must discover the right words or actions so they will move toward us and let us and the gospel into their lives.

Recognizing That Evangelism Is a Process

Dick Innes wrote a book titled *I Hate Witnessing*. Innes does not oppose witnessing in the biblical sense, but he opposes the forcing of any particular program without consideration of where the individual may be.

A chapter titled "One Step at a Time" in Innes' book has a chart showing the Spiritual Decision Process (see next page). The minus side of the scale represents the nonbeliever. At minus eight an individual has an awareness of a "Supreme Being but no effective knowledge or understanding of the gospel." Zero represents the point at which a person actually makes a commitment to Christ and becomes a Christian. The plus side of the scale is for the Christian. It represents his or her spiritual growth and maturity.[3]

+8	
+7	
+6	
+5	Post-decision evaluation, fellowship in the church, Christian growth and maturity, fruits and gifts of the Spirit, discipleship, etc.
+4	
+3	
+2	
+1	
0	Point of conversion or new birth
-1	Repentance and faith in Christ
-2	Decision to act
-3	Personal problem/need recognition
-4	
-5	Increased understanding of the gospel and its implications
-6	
-7	Belief in a Supreme Being but no effective understanding of the gospel
-8	

John A. Mayer, Religion Information Services ©1997. Used with permission.

Evangelism doesn't take place only at the point a person makes a commitment to Christ. Every action, influence, or word that draws a person even a half-step closer to Christ is evangelism. It is a process, not an event. It most often occurs through our relationships. The apostle Paul said God is the Father of compassion and comfort, and He "comforts us in all our troubles, so that we can comfort those in any trouble with the comfort we ourselves have received from God" (2 Corinthians 2:4).

Evangelizing is helping others just as we were helped. The situation may be different from ours, but the need for help is the same as we had when God sent someone to lead us to salvation. It is right that we should be helping because we know the One who can solve all problems. Our caring and loving attitude will draw people from the precipice overlooking hell to the safety of the Cross.

Looking for the Keys

Paul requested that the Colossians pray that God would "open a door for our message, so that we may proclaim the mystery of Christ" (Colossians 4:3).

"God, who ... through us spreads everywhere the fragrance of the knowledge of him" (2 Corinthians 2:14). We need to pray not only for keys of opportunity, but also for open eyes to see them. Jesus asked the people of His day, "'Do you have eyes but fail to see, and ears but fail to hear?'" (Mark 8:18).

Paul encourages us to "Be wise in the way you act toward outsiders; make the most of every opportunity" (Colossians 4:5). From time to time we all walk past opportunities. We can be wise and discover keys for reaching people with the gospel as we open our eyes to see and our ears to hear

- what community leaders are saying
- what school officials are saying
- what newspaper editorials are saying about various aspects of the community
- what parents are saying
- what those inside and those outside the church are saying

As you listen you will hear a cry for help and discover keys to people's lives and to your community. Your list would probably look something like the following, which many communities are saying:

- We are lonely and need a friend.
- We are afraid of the future due to uncertain times.
- We need help in raising our children.
- We need someone to work with our boys because they have no stable role models.
- We need some wholesome activities for our teens.
- We need someone we can trust. Can we trust the church?
- We need something that gives us hope.
- We want to know if someone really cares about us.
- We are looking for reality.

LONELINESS

In his 1996 Minneapolis Crusade, Billy Graham said, "They had a conference in New York of psychiatrists recently and they dealt with the problem of loneliness, and they agreed that loneliness was one of the greatest problems that young people face today. The Associated Press reported that the Number 1 problem in America today among young people is loneliness. And it's one of the supreme human problems of society."[4]

The world population is growing rapidly, and personal isolation is keeping pace with it. Several problems come with the population growth. TV provides entertainment, and people tend to stay home and watch it. They don't socialize as much as they might have in the past. With crime rates soaring, people cut themselves off from society to stay at home—a safe place. Computers provide access to the world through the Internet; still, the people using them are isolated and anonymous. They are not truly socializing. Finding a key to alleviate the loneliness of these people, created by their isolation, will provide a path to reaching them with God's love.

76 TAKING THE FIELD

FEAR OF THE FUTURE

Every newspaper speaks to us of the uncertainty of our times. Corporate cutbacks and downsizing have cut into financial security. The AIDS epidemic, rising medical costs, and conflicting messages regarding the future of health care and Social Security take their toll on the American sense of well-being. World conditions of famine, war, and damaging weather can cause uncertainty in our lives; the breakdown of the family and rampant crime add to the uneasiness of what tomorrow will bring.

The surety of God's Word is a key for giving assurance to the people who fear the future. All else may and will change, but God's Word is eternal. People need the peace in their lives that only God can give. We have Jesus' own promise, "'My peace I give you.... Do not let your hearts be troubled and do not be afraid'" (John 14:27).

HELP IN CHILD REARING

Many children are rebellious, disrespectful, and disobedient toward all authority. Parents simply do not know what to do. They feel their situations are out of control. They find themselves unable to set boundaries or to provide even the basic emotional support to help their children become healthy, productive members of society.

With self-centered, tired, or too-busy parents, too many children are missing the reassurance of affection and the discipline of love they need at home. Broken homes, broken families, and broken relationships have resulted in single-parent homes and poverty for children. Never-married and divorced mothers, fathers who are becoming primary caregivers, and others who feel inadequate to parent are searching for help to know how to rear their children. Their need for training is a key to reach these hurting parents and their children.

ROLE MODELS FOR BOYS

Divorce, absentee fathers, or never-married mothers leave boys without role models and girls without adequate interaction with a male parent for normal relational development. Cries for help have been coming from leaders of our cities asking that the church become involved in helping provide role models, particularly for boys who are growing up without fathers. While risk does exist if we do not take precautions on behalf of those who deal with children, we should not avoid this opportunity to reach people in need.

ACTIVITIES FOR TEENS

The participants at one community committee meeting of concerned parents were people from all walks of life. They voiced an overwhelming concern about the teen drinking and partying that was occurring after the school activities. Could a key for reaching these families be your church stepping in and providing something that would involve the energy, free time, and interest of teens? What activities would appeal to their need for independence, their search for friends, and their desire to express their fears and hopes?

SOMEONE TO TRUST

People are saying, "We need someone we can trust. Can we trust the church?" Integrity in leadership is more important now than ever. Local, state, and federal government leaders have fallen far short of being trustworthy. Their word is true for them for that moment; it readily changes with the situation. The church should be the safest place in town. Of all places, it should be the one place where people can have confidence in the words and actions of the people there. Are we doing all we can to be that kind of person? Are we people of integrity? Do we keep our word? Do we obey God's Word and always try to do what's right, not just what we want for us? If the community learns that truth and integrity are the backbone of our church, we are in a key position to reach those who need someone they can trust.

PROMISE OF HOPE

Leaders often promise whatever they think people want to hear. People believe them because they hope those leaders will somehow make a difference in their lives. No matter what leaders can achieve for us, there is no permanent hope in this world or its leaders. The only sure hope is in God. He assures us with this promise, "'I know the plans I have for you . . . plans to give you hope and a future'" (Jeremiah 29:11).

Only the church can offer absolute hope, for our God is a God of promise and of hope. "Since we have been justified through faith, we have peace with God through our Lord Jesus Christ, through whom we have gained access by faith into this grace in which we now stand. And we rejoice in the hope of the glory of God" (Romans 5:1,2). People want assurance of hope. This is a key to an opportunity for Christians to reach out to those who are asking, "Is this all there is?"

SOMEONE TO CARE

People like to feel they are important. No one wants to be just a number or a statistic. People are drawn to those who make them feel important, showing care for their needs and for them. No one cares for us like Jesus. God cares for each of us individually, so much so that He numbers the very hairs of our head (Matthew 10:30). He sent His only Son to suffer and die in our place to show how important each person is to Him. True caring is a key to touching people who need someone to care.

SOMETHING REAL

Things that are real draw people and stand the test of time. Are we for real? Are we burdened for the lost so that we are willing to reach out to people because of their need and not for our own self-interest? Are we willing to be the "Good Samaritan," not expecting anything in return for our contribution to meet a need in someone's life?

Touching Where We Can

The areas listed are just a few of the possibilities for open doors of ministry for the church. Involvement in any of these provides not only a key for entry into an individual's heart but also an opportunity for the church to touch the community. Perhaps you, as an individual, or your particular ministry can reach out in one or more of these areas.

TOUCHING THROUGH ACTIONS

When we were first married, my wife worked for a man who was intolerant of anything religious, other than his own particular denomination. He would get noticeably angry if anything religious came up at the office. Sensing her supervisor's antagonism and realizing this was not the place to say anything about God, my wife simply went about her work in a conscientious manner.

Several months after she left that job, I was visiting someone in the hospital in a neighboring community and ran into this man. I greeted him, called him by name, and asked him what brought him to the hospital. Tears came to his eyes and he replied, "I'm here because my father is dying."

I placed a hand on his shoulder and said, "Would you mind if I had a word of prayer with you for your dad?" I prayed simply that God would touch his father and also comfort and strengthen their family during this difficult time. That was all I felt was appropriate to do at that moment.

This story illustrates a principle I have found to be true. *A man who would reject you if you tried to talk to him about God will let you minister to him in a time of need.*

Although we had known him for some time, this encounter

served as a key to this man's life. God gave us favor with him and brought him back into our lives on several occasions after that. It was exciting to see how his life began to be surrounded by other Christian influences. His daughter went away to college and "just happened" to be placed in a room with a girl their family dearly loved, a pastor's daughter.

The end of the story has not yet been written, but I am confident that I did my part at that particular time in the harvest process going on in his life.

Your community, though it may be very resistant to the gospel, still has many doors of ministry for the church. Meeting needs is the key that will open the doors to hearts.

Touching Through Words

Paul asked for prayer not only for a door of opportunity to be opened for him, but also that he would proclaim the message clearly (Colossians 4:3,4). Paul was not only concerned that he would say the right thing when the opportunity arose, but also that the Colossians would do the same. He instructs them to "be wise in the way you act toward outsiders; make the most of every opportunity. Let your conversation be always full of grace, seasoned with salt, so that you may know how to answer everyone" (Colossians 4:5,6). This verse implies that the world is looking for answers and that we need to be wise in the answers we offer.

Someone said recently, "The church is often good at answering questions no one is asking." It is possible to be so concerned with getting our message across that we do not hear what others are asking. In doing so, we can overlook the key that would open their hearts and give us entry into their lives.

I picked up an article in the newspaper recently about a small town that had undergone a series of tragedies within a short time. My first thought was, *Will our church be able to play a part in bringing healing to that hurting community?* This article contained several comments as to how people were dealing with these tragedies. One of the comments grabbed my attention: "What have we done to deserve all this?"

That was a question I had heard before from nonbelievers. My mind went back to a school conference my wife and I attended when one of our sons was in elementary school. At the close of the conference time, the teacher said, "You know, I love your son like he was my own. I don't know if you realize it or not, but I had a son with the same name as your son's. He was killed in a car accident last year." She began to weep, then walked over and closed the door to her room and continued. "Your son reminds me a lot of my son at that age." She looked and me and said, "You're a minister. Maybe you can help me. I have asked God a million times what I have ever done that was so terrible that He would take my son away from me."

We shared with her that we do not have answers for why some things happen, but one thing we did know: God was not punishing her. God was there to provide comfort and help for her during that difficult time in her life.

This experience was a key into her heart and ended up opening up the hearts of many in the school system to us, to our church, and to what God had for them.

Targeting Receptive People

Rick Warren, in *The Purpose Driven Church,* identifies two main categories of people who are most receptive to the gospel: "People in transition and people under tension. God uses both change and pain to get people's attention and make them receptive to the Gospel.

"Any time someone experiences major change, whether positive or negative, it seems to create a hunger for spiritual stability. . . . people are more receptive to the Gospel when they face changes like a new marriage, a new baby, a new home, a new job, or a new school. That is why churches generally grow faster in new communities where residents are continually moving in than in older communities where people have lived for forty years."[5]

Here is Warren's list of the 10 most receptive groups in his ministry:

1. Second-time visitors to the church
2. Close friends and relatives of new converts
3. People going through a divorce
4. Those who feel their need for a recovery program (alcohol, drugs, sexual, and so forth)
5. First-time parents
6. The terminally ill and their families
7. Couples with major marriage problems
8. Parents with problem children
9. Recently unemployed or those with major financial problems
10. New residents in the community[6]

Creating Opportunities

Look again at the list of most receptive groups. There are at least 10 possibilities of groups of people to reach. People with specific problems and needs are in every community. How many can you check off that you are aware of in your community? How will you reach them?

Looking at Who Is Missing

Sitting on the platform one Sunday morning, I looked out at the people who were gathered there to see who, if anyone, was missing. It didn't take too long to see that everyone (all 13 of us—two families plus my wife and I) had made it to church that day. Then it dawned on me that though everyone had come, we were missing everybody, for both of those families there that morning lived outside the city limits. That meant not one person from that city was attending our church. Now, that is not an encouraging thought—"We are missing everybody." But it was true. We realized that if there was ever going to be a church of more than 13 outsiders, we were going to have to win some of those from inside the community to the Lord.

There were no other churches of our fellowship nearby for people to transfer from to come to our church. In addition, we lived in an area that people rarely moved in to. There was only one way we would have growth and that was to reach people in the city itself.

Venturing Into the Lost World

We can create opportunities by deliberately venturing into the lost world. Lee Strobel, in his book *Inside the Mind of Unchurched Harry and Mary,* says, "One effective strategy is to specifically work at retaining contact with some of your unchurched friends you had before you became a committed Christian."[7] He also suggests patronizing the same shops, restaurants, and gas stations in order to get to know the salespeople, waiters and waitresses, and attendants. Becoming active in civic and school organizations and joining park district softball leagues would also provide opportunities to develop social contacts with unchurched people.

A pastor who recently moved into a community to pioneer a church used one of these suggestions. He lived in the area for four months before beginning church services, getting acquainted with the people in the community. During this period of time he regularly frequented a certain restaurant, becoming friendly with the owners, workers, and regular customers.

After about 8 months, he walked into the restaurant and the place was filled with party balloons. He asked, "What's going on? Whose birthday?" He was surprised to find out they were celebrating his birthday. This pastor had developed relationships that made it possible for his church to thrive in that community.

DEVELOPING CHURCH MINISTRIES

Do you remember the illustration of the 2-year-old on the roof, the one about making people want to come to Jesus? In Luke 14:23, Jesus said, "'Go out to the roads and country lanes and make them come in, so that my house will be full.'" As much as we may desire to do so, we cannot force people against their will. This verse means we must find a way to make them want to come.

A class or church can develop ministries or activities ranging from the very lowest-key approaches to high-gear evangelistic meetings that will draw people into the Kingdom or "make them want to come." There are a variety of people in every community who will respond to one of the approaches. There is no one best way; the best way is the way that works.

Rick Warren points out that Jesus had no standard method for evangelizing. He approached people by starting where they were. He used illustrations familiar to the people—farm stories for farmers, fishing illustrations for fishermen, and sheep parables for shepherds.

He writes, "I've noticed that whenever I go fishing the fish don't automatically jump into my boat or throw themselves on the shore for me. Their culture (underwater) is very different from mine (air). It takes intentional effort on my part to make contact with fish. Somehow I must figure out how to get the bait right in front of their nose in their culture.

"Churches that expect the unchurched to show up simply because they build a building and hang out a 'We're Open' sign are indulging themselves. People don't voluntarily jump into your boat. You must penetrate their culture."[8]

In his book *Evangelism That Works,* George Barna suggests three ways that non-Christians will allow themselves to be initially approached:[9]

- Churched people build caring relationships with nonchurched people, then invite them to church.

- The church sponsors events that interest unchurched people and invites them to participate, such as sports leagues, community social events and assistance projects, concerts, and seminars. Involvement in these events provide opportunity to invite the people to church activities.
- Sending brochures to people to inform them about the church and invite them to attend. The following factors greatly affect the results of this approach: The quality, timing, and nature of the brochure; the recipients; the region; and the church itself.

Anything that draws new people into our church is a key to opening a door in their lives. We can take advantage of the calendar. People who would not attend church any other time of the year will come to Christmas and Easter activities.

I know of one church that has 20,000 people coming each year to its Christmas production. Through this ministry, unsaved people come and hear the gospel presented in a very clear way. Many of them respond and end up as part of that church.

In his same book, George Barna gives a sampling of events used by churches focusing on evangelism:

- Christmas or Easter musical
- Picnics, athletic events, concerts
- Thanksgiving meal for the needy
- Seminars, community forums
- Youth rallies or sports parties
- Showing of an evangelistic movie
- Businesspeople's luncheons
- Days designed for bringing friends
- Community fair or carnival
- Evangelistic crusades
- Sports clinics
- Mother's Day or Father's Day banquet
- Community service projects
- Neighborhood or block parties

- Halloween alternative event
- Planting new churches
- Telephone hot line for counseling
- Live nativity scene for the Christmas season
- Community-wide marathon
- Valentine's Day banquet
- Art fair
- Ethnic/cultural celebrations
- Passover celebration
- Wild-game banquet

Such events are in addition to ongoing ministries at churches whose primary thrust is evangelistic.

Among the outreach activities that have sharing the gospel as their main objective are affinity group ministries, such as to prisoners, convalescents, unwed mothers, homeless children, non-English-speaking persons, mothers of preschoolers; seasonal programs, such as sports leagues or vacation Bible school; regularly offered classes, such as Sunday school, introductory Christianity, 12-step programs; evangelistic small groups; and other miscellaneous kinds of efforts, such as community development, employment training, and bus ministry.[10]

The list of possible events is included not to overwhelm those in small churches but rather to stimulate thinking. We should move past what we cannot do and find the key our church can use to open the doors to reach the lost.

Be especially sensitive to crises that may affect the nation and, in particular, your area. During the Gulf War several years ago, for example, people in America were very open to prayer vigils. There are also things you can do outside your church walls. For example, your class or group could volunteer for a community project. Anything that moves you outside the walls of your church and into the community can serve as a key to open the door of people's hearts.

God does not want "anyone to perish, but everyone to come

to repentance" (2 Peter 3:9). We must, by every means possible, compel the lost to come into a relationship with Christ. People without Jesus are left on the precipice, shivering under their burdens of cares and hurts. Will we reach them in time? Will we persuade them to come to safety?

Endnotes

[1] Rick Warren, *The Purpose Driven Church* (Grand Rapids, Mich.: Zondervan Publishing House, 1995), 185.

[2] Ibid., 181.

[3] Dick Innes, *I Hate Witnessing* (Ventura, Calif.: Vision House, 1978), 128–32.

[4] Billy Graham, as quoted in the Minneapolis *Star Tribune*, June 21, 1996.

[5] Warren, *The Purpose Driven Church,* 182.

[6] Ibid., 183.

[7] Lee Strobel, *Inside the World of Unchurched Harry and Mary* (Grand Rapids, Mich.: Zondervan Publishing House, 1993), 86.

[8] Warren, *The Purpose Driven Church,* 196.

[9] George Barna, *Evangelism That Works* (Ventura, Calif.: Regal Books, 1995), 64.

[10] Ibid., 95.

6
Relating to the Community

There is a difference between building a church and touching a community. It is possible to have a large church that has a very limited impact on society because it exists for itself. Most of the time, energy, and resources of the parishioners are spent on those in the church itself. This is the beginning stage of a declining church.

It is also possible to have a small church, particularly in a smaller community, that has kept a focus outside its walls and is touching the community.

The church's impact on its community is determined to a great extent by how it relates to the community. Just as individuals relate to each other, the church has a relationship with its community.

The Church's Relationships

A STORMY RELATIONSHIP

Some churches pit themselves against the city, taking strong and vocal positions on many issues. This stormy relationship can polarize the community. Although a church may experience growth with this type of approach, it may also make needless enemies of large sections of the population.

When we view the unsaved as the enemy, psychologically we alienate them. Satan is the enemy. Unsaved people are not the enemy; they are victims of the enemy, and they need us.

A Silent Relationship

The reactions people give when asked where a particular church is located in their city tells a great deal about its relationship to the city. The church can have a silent relationship whereby the community, as a whole, is not even aware that the church exists. To be effective, the community has to at least know the church is there.

A Loving Relationship

The church can have a loving relationship with the community. This does not mean the church condones the sin in the city, but rather that it concentrates on loving the sinner and becomes known as a place to turn to in time of difficulty. This type of church operates out of a love for a given area, and it often takes years to develop this type of relationship to an effective degree.

A Crisis-Solving Relationship

In some circumstances God opens the hearts of people in a city immediately. Usually, this occurs in places of extreme need. The crisis in cities and towns is apparent; we see more youth committing more serious crimes at younger and younger ages. Many of the programs designed to solve these problems are now in disarray.

When the problems a city faces become so overwhelming and those in authority realize they have no answers, they often ask the church to become involved in solving some of the problems. This is happening in many cities and opens doors of opportunity for the church. They may not be doors we would desire to have open to us; however, as we take advantage of those that are open, we find they lead to other open doors, which in turn often lead to the doors that open people's hearts.

Relating to the Community

Our answers to the following questions will give us insight into how we relate to our community.

A CLUB OR A HOSPITAL

Do we see the church primarily as an exclusive club for Christians or as a hospital for the hurting? We probably would answer, "A hospital for the hurting," for we remember that Jesus said, "'It is not the healthy who need a doctor, but the sick. I have not come to call the righteous, but sinners'" (Mark 2:17). But even though we say hospital, our actions may tell a different story.

A hospital is built to take care of needs. It has an emergency room, intensive care area, cardiac care area, nursery area, and other specific and individual rooms; all areas are organized to take care of people's needs. The focus is on helping the hurting, not on the staff.

A country club is usually exclusive. Gaining membership in it can be difficult. It exists primarily for the benefit of its current members. Churches that are like country clubs effectively keep out new or unwelcome members.

A FORTRESS OR A FORT

Do we view the church primarily as a fortress or a fort? The more we seclude ourselves from the rest of the world, the less effect we have on that world and the more troubled that world becomes.

When we see ourselves as the persecuted few and everyone outside the church as the enemy, we tend to isolate ourselves in the fortress to protect ourselves and our children. Venturing out into the world often is in the form of an attack. Instead, the church should be viewed as the fort that people run to for safety from danger—a place of acceptance, comfort, and help.

POSITIVE OR NEGATIVE TEACHING

Are the preaching and teaching basically positive or negative?

Several years ago, during the height of the charismatic renewal, when many people in all denominations were coming to personal faith and experiencing the baptism in the Holy Spirit, a well-known evangelist published a series of articles denouncing the Catholic Church and stating that he did not believe that anyone could stay in the Catholic Church and still be a Christian. Many of those involved in the renewal that the Catholic Church was experiencing threw up walls of resistance to this negative teaching.

About that same time, another pastor handled the pope's visit to his city in a positive way. He placed posters all over town telling people to come to his church and hear him speak on the topic, "Why I Love the Virgin Mary." Catholics flocked to his church, bought tapes, and took them home to their priests. The points of his message were: "I love the Virgin Mary because she was the Mother of Jesus. I love the Virgin Mary because she recognized that Jesus was the only way to salvation. I love the Virgin Mary because she recognized the importance of obedience, for she said, '"Do whatever he tells you"'" (John 2:5). He preached a noncompromising, positive message that could be received by the same kind of people who rejected the negative teaching.

These two methods of handling a similar situation show that we can get the same message across in two different ways; however, one way closed doors and alienated people and the other kept the door open.

92 TAKING THE FIELD

> Nearly three quarters of a century ago, advertising pioneer, John Caples . . . in his classic book, *Tested Advertising Methods,* . . . talked about a split-run for a product still around today, Milk Bone dog snacks. Both ads offered a free gift pack of Milk Bone snacks. Both ads carried the same message: Feeding your dog table scraps in summer is dangerous. One ad used a negative appeal, the other a positive one.
> Ad A: "Don't Poison Your Dog!"
> Ad B: "Keep Your Dog Safe This Summer"
> When the coupons were counted, the advertiser found that Ad B had pulled 58% more responses.

The advertising company looked at those responses and decided not to use Ad A, but to use Ad B.[1]

"'The people of this world are more shrewd in dealing with their own kind than are the people of light'" (Luke 16:8). Are we wise enough to appeal to the unsaved in positive ways so they will want to come to God?

Focus on Unbelievers

Is our ministry to Christians only or do we also focus on the unconverted? How do we want our community to view us?

When we speak of seeking to touch the heart of a city, we are not referring to a goal of acceptance, for that might involve compromising our message. We are referring to our reputation. This reputation is developed by our attitudes and our actions that minimize antagonism in order to maximize changed lives. "'Let your light so shine before men, that they may see your good deeds and praise your Father in heaven'" (Matthew 5:16).

A church's reputation in the community is determined by the reputation of its leadership, its written and unwritten policies, and its actions carried out through its various ministries. Paul reminded Timothy that those in leadership in the church "must also have a good reputation with outsiders"

(1 Timothy 3:7). As leaders we must watch the little things in our lives, but not focus on the little things in the lives of the people we are trying to reach.

Rick Warren says this about the church's attitude toward unbelievers: "If your church is serious about reaching the unchurched, you must be willing to put up with people who have a lot of problems. Fishing is often messy and smelly. Many churches want the fish they catch to be already scaled, gutted, cleaned, and cooked. That is why they never reach anyone."[2]

Some churches have wonderful reputations in their communities as places where leaders not only walk with integrity, but where the church itself is known as an accepting place where people can turn for help and guidance.

ATTITUDE TOWARD OTHER MINISTRIES

What is our attitude toward other ministries?

We need to determine to build the Kingdom, not just our church. We may be tempted to be concerned about only our particular area of responsibility, to the exclusion of all others. But we are here to build the body of Christ, not just our particular ministry.

When we are able to accept that an individual we have invested in may choose to attend another church or another class, and we can bless that individual and that ministry, we have discovered a key to God's blessing. When it does not matter who does the reaping from our planting and watering or who gets the credit for Kingdom growth, it is amazing what can be accomplished.

Adopting Positive Principles

A church that touches the hearts of people in a community has individuals and ministries that operate according to the following principles.

LOVING THE COMMUNITY

We must love not only our particular ministry and church, but also the community where we are living. Touching a community begins with a love for that community and the individuals who live and work there. This is the beginning and most important point of ministry. If we do everything else and do not love, we are "only a resounding gong or a clanging cymbal" (1 Corinthians 13:1).

Scripture teaches that all the Law and the Prophets are based on the commandments of loving God and loving our neighbor (Matthew 22:37–40). "Love does no harm to its neighbor. Therefore love is the fulfillment of the law" (Romans 13:10). In the same manner that love enables an individual to fulfill the whole Law, love enables an individual to do the right thing in reaching and touching people. When we operate out of love and concern for an individual, we tend to do the right things.

Love is very appealing; it's what draws people to us. People want to be loved. They do not want to be somebody's project.

Besides loving people, we must work at having a right attitude toward our community in general. It is possible to live in an area and be very negative about it. People have a sense of pride about their community. If we want to touch that neighborhood and community for God, they need to sense that we love them and that community. This is particularly important for those who are new to an area. We will not effectively touch a community that we do not love.

BUILDING RELATIONSHIPS

We must develop a philosophy and lifestyle of never closing a door in our personal relationships with people and of making friends wherever we go. Any friend of ours becomes a friend of our ministry. Even if they personally would never darken the door of our church, if they know us, like us, and trust us, they are more likely to allow their children to attend or to say a good word about our church should any of their friends or relatives start to attend.

In one-on-one relationships, it is a good policy not to push any issue so far that we would not have an opportunity to talk with that person again. We do not have to do it all in one day. Earl Palmer, writing in the book *Growing Your Church Through Evangelism and Outreach,* states, "The idea that this is my only chance to talk to a person is a great detriment."[3] God does not work with us in that manner. He leads us one step at a time.

If we have a heart that desires to reach the lost, the Holy Spirit will be faithful to show us those times we need to press the issue in our one-on-one relationships with people.

BEING A POSITIVE INFLUENCE

We must believe that God has placed us in our neighborhood or job to be a positive influence. Believing we are sent to our responsibilities and being faithful to those responsibilities, we determine to become loving, caring, good neighbors, and reliable and honest employees. By our actions we earn the right to be heard, because our actions speak much more forcefully than our words.

The closer our relationship with an individual is on a daily basis, the more we need to speak the gospel by our life rather than by our words. Peter gave this advice to women trying to win their husbands, "If any of them do not believe the word, they may be won over without words by the behavior of their wives" (1 Peter 3:1). This principle is true for all close relationships. If the individual is not responsive to the gospel, we need to back off, love unconditionally, and continue to pray that God will open the person's heart. Then, we need to live carefully and prayerfully before that individual, speaking when and if the Holy Spirit impresses us to say something.

DEVELOPING A PHILOSOPHY OF EVANGELISM

We must develop a philosophy of evangelism that attracts more people than it turns away. Some methods will win one or two, but in the process may alienate a city. It is easier to reach people if we do not have to tear down barriers first. We want to win the war, not just one battle. We will not win those we alienate by our methods.

George Barna identified "several activities that are more likely to turn off the unchurched rather than to get them interested or excited about your church. Calling people on the telephone to invite them, commonly known as telemarketing, leaves a bad taste in the mouth of most nonchurched people. A relative handful of people might follow through and attend, but the negative fallout is so substantial that telemarketing often represents bad stewardship and shortsighted evangelism.

"The other tactic that has as great a potential to sour nonchurched adults on a church experience is visiting their homes uninvited. This act creates a measurable hostility toward the Christian faith and its churches."[4]

Aggressive contacts, such as telemarketing or home visitation, bring negative reactions from the nonchurched for the same reasons that telemarketing or door-to-door salespeople evoke negative responses. Such efforts as telemarketing and uninvited home visitations send the message that their privacy and their time are less important than our agenda. We are imposing our beliefs and values on them through these approaches.

Having a life-changing experience with God, through Jesus' sacrifice on the cross, is more important than whatever people might be doing when the contact is made. But nonchurched people see the telemarketing or visiting their homes uninvited as simply another example of religious fanatics forcing their views on other people.

Developing a Philosophy of Ministry

We must develop a positive philosophy of ministry. How will we deal with the evil that is around us? Should we fight it? Should we overlook it? Are we compromising if we do not point out the wrong?

These are hard questions. But how they are answered will

have a great deal to do with our influence on our community. One of Aesop's fables contains a truth that can give an answer to these questions.

The wind and the sun were arguing over who was the most powerful. The wind looked down and saw a man walking, wearing a heavy coat. He threw out the challenge to the sun that the most powerful of the two would be the one who could get the man to take off his coat.

The wind blew and blew, but the man just wrapped his coat around him and held it tighter. The wind kept blowing, but the man still held to his coat, though the force of the wind was almost shredding it.

The sun then took its turn. It smiled and smiled. Soon the man, of his own free will, took off the coat and folded it across his arm as the warmth of the sun continued to shine on him.

We will have to decide if the basic thrust of our community involvement will be trying to force change or if we will concentrate on winning people and letting God do the changing in their lives.

We can learn much from looking at how Paul appealed to the Athenians on Mars Hill. Scripture tells us "he was greatly distressed to see that the city was full of idols" (Acts 17:16). Paul did not organize a picket or a boycott or start preaching about the evil of worshiping idols. Rather, he said, "'Men of Athens! I see that in every way you are very religious. For as I walked around and looked carefully at your objects of worship, I even found an altar with this inscription: TO AN UNKNOWN GOD. Now what you worship as something unknown I am going to proclaim to you'" (Acts 17:22).

Paul noticed their culture. He did not condemn them; he found a point from which he could communicate the truth of the gospel to them.

GETTING INVOLVED IN THE COMMUNITY

We must find an area of the community to be involved in in a positive way. Get involved in some area of natural interest, such as coaching, helping chaperone groups, or tutoring. The list is endless. We must find something that will put us in contact with people outside our church circle. If our desire is to reach lost people, we will find that the friendships developed in those types of settings often prove to be more than chance meetings. They are divine appointments; they are opportunities to touch people's lives.

Our natural interests open doors to ways of getting involved in our community. If we have children, the activities they are involved in offer us ways to become a positive part of that community. Their schools and extracurricular activities are wonderful places to meet people.

Getting involved in the parent-teacher group, not for the purpose of picking out what is wrong with the system, but to help out where we can, will open doors of opportunity that might not open any other way.

When we walk into lost people's lives to work beside them in the community, we need to look beyond their sin to reaching the sinner. We should not be surprised when sinners sin; that's what sinners do. It is the Holy Spirit's job to convict of sin. It is our job to be available as a witness to what God can do in our lives. Getting involved in the community is one way of being where people who need God are.

Providing Entries Into the Church

We must provide some nonthreatening entries into our church or ministry. Not all people are at the same point in their spiritual journey. We need to design entry opportunities for all positions on the spectrum, from those who are trained and eager to begin working for God to those who are still questioning about God.

> A key lesson from our study of evangelistic churches is that a church that is serious about reaching people with the gospel must have a multitude of alternatives or entry points accessi-

ble to nonbelievers who are exploring the value of Christianity. Reliance upon a single means or entry point designed to usher people into a lasting relationship with Christ is insufficient.

Further research points out ... that no single church or evangelistic strategy is capable of reaching every nonbeliever within the community.[5]

Some churches provide minimum appeal and opportunities. Other churches have a great variety of opportunities, ranging from multiple classes to day care to programs and events in the church for adults and children. Special speakers, sports groups, or a ladies' dinner appeal to a variety of people in the community. Providing entry into the church through people's interests involves trying a variety of things in order to draw in as many nonchurched people as possible in nonthreatening ways.

Fostering the Right Attitude

We must foster an attitude in our church that encourages people who are strong Christians to become involved in the community.

The church can become such a busy place that it takes all of our time and energy. We may need to look at our schedules and plan times to spend with lost people. Everyone does not have to be at every function all the time. We need to teach faithfulness, but somehow allow Christians to be involved in the community and bless them for that involvement rather than making them feel guilty if they miss some activity at the church.

Earning Credibility

We must earn the right to be heard. George Barna reminds us that people of this generation do not automatically accept and believe today. "In a society that breeds mistrust, skepticism, and the assumption of intentional deceit by people who are pursuing their personal agendas, it is to be expected that young people will show little willingness to accept what others are recommending to them without thoroughly testing those beliefs."[6]

Credibility is earned by our positive interaction with the people in our community. As we love them, build relationships with them, exert a positive influence, communicate the gospel through acceptable methods, get involved in the community, offer a variety of opportunities that draw people to the church, and have a right attitude about spending time outside the church with the lost we are trying to reach, our integrity is seen, our love is an example, and our words become real. That's credibility.

The challenges involved in touching a community are great, but the reward of winning souls is greater.

Endnotes

[1]Stann Rapp and Thomas Collins, "The New Maxi Marketing," *Success Magazine,* April 1996, 43ff.

[2]Rick Warren, *The Purpose Driven Church* (Grand Rapids, Mich.: Zondervan Publishing House, 1995), 198.

[3]Earl Palmer, *Growing Your Church Through Evangelism and Outreach* (New York: Moorings, A Division of Ballentine Publishing Group, Random House, Inc., 1993), 12.

[4]George Barna, *Evangelism That Works* (Ventura, Calif.: Regal Books, 1995), 63–64.

[5]Ibid., 104.

[6]Ibid., 108, 109.

7
Seeing Beyond Circumstances

We need to be ambassadors for Christ. We need to hear God's voice. We need to speak for God. We need to find keys into people's lives and ways to influence our community. The process of creative thinking can be used to develop our ministries to accomplish these goals.

Creative Thinking

In his book titled *Six Thinking Hats,* Edward de Bono, a teacher of creative thinking skills, suggests that people think of wearing six different hats in going through the creative process. *It is very important that the first four are done one at a time and in proper sequence.*

1. Green hat—brainstorming which consists of the gathering of ideas. No positive or negative comments allowed at this time.
2. Yellow hat—listing of positive constructive thoughts as to why an idea might work.
3. Black hat—listing of logical negative thoughts about an idea.
4. Red hat—feeling and emotion. Even if an idea is a good one, if people do not like it, it probably will not succeed.
5. White hat—facts, figures, and objective information that can be used at any time.

6. Blue hat—worn by the person in charge who controls the thinking steps.[1]

God would like to open our spiritual eyes and give us new vision for our areas of ministry, for our churches, and for our communities. We must look beyond our present circumstances and surroundings and see our communities, neighborhoods, and ministries as God sees them.

Seeing the Potential

The devil has done a good job of blinding our eyes to our own potential and to the possibilities around us. As a result, we may be overlooking great opportunities that lay before us.

Hagar was wearing the black hat. She could not see the well that could provide water to save both her life and that of her son, Ishmael. She saw only her present desperate circumstances until "God opened her eyes and she saw a well of water. So she went and filled the skin with water and gave the boy a drink" (Genesis 21:19).

Elisha's servant was also wearing the black hat. "'Oh, my lord, what shall we do?'" Elisha's servant cried when he saw the multitude of Syrian horses and chariots surrounding the city of Dothan to capture the prophet Elisha. "'Don't be afraid,'" Elisha answered. "'Those who are with us are more than those who are with them.'" Then Elisha, who may have been wearing the white hat, prayed, "'O Lord, open his eyes so he may see.' Then the Lord opened the servant's eyes, and he looked and saw the hills full of horses and chariots of fire all around Elisha" (2 Kings 6:15–17).

A relevant quote, attributed to Marcel Proust, says, "The real voyage of discovery consists not in seeking new landscapes but in having new eyes."

Having a Vision

A vision is so powerful that the writer of Proverbs tells us, "Where there is no vision, the people perish" (29:18, KJV). Rick

Warren in *The Purpose Driven Church* drives this truth home in reminding us, "Where there is no vision in the church, people leave for another parish."[2]

George Bernard Shaw wrote, "I am a dreamer. Some men see things as they are, and ask why; I dream of things that never were, and ask why not?"[3] Bobby Kennedy used Shaw's words to eloquently campaign for the presidency of the United States. Perhaps Martin Luther King wore the yellow hat when he challenged our nation and rallied people behind him with the words "I have a dream."

Our vision dominates our life and our ministry. How we perceive things determines what we will do. Proverbs 27:19 says, "A man's heart reflects the man." What a man thinks he eventually becomes.

STATING THE VISION

Many churches and ministries within the church have recently spent time writing and rewriting vision statements. The vision statement spells out the group's reason for being. Usually this statement includes thoughts something like this: "We believe we are here to worship God, encourage each other, and influence our world for Jesus Christ." Most vision statements are some variation of that theme.

A vision statement for a boys group, a girls group, or a teen program may emphasize reaching, teaching, and keeping boys, girls, or teens involved in that particular group. If you have not done so, take the time to sit down and write out a vision statement for your class or ministry.

ACCOMPLISHING THE VISION

A vision statement is only the starting point. The question then needs to be asked, "How can we best accomplish this vision with our talents, personality, and resources?" This is where creativity enters.

Our mission requires us to envision ways to bring in the lost and to nurture them. God has given us creativity to help us accomplish this task. Although most evangelism has its basis in the development of one-on-one relationships with people, a church or a class can do many things to reach those outside its walls.

In his study of churches geared toward evangelism, George Barna discovered that leaders "focusing on evangelism intentionally carve hours out of their busy schedules to simply dream about how to reach the non-reached community . . . ."

"Millions of nonbelievers need to be reached with the gospel. It will take every bit of energy, creativity, determination and prayer that we can muster to create effective mechanisms for introducing these people to the real Jesus Christ."[4]

Anointed creativity in a church or classroom setting is a must for effectively touching those individuals to whom you are already ministering and for reaching those outside the walls of the church.

Steps of Creativity

In an article titled "The Well-Fed Imagination," Robert J. Morgan suggests the following five steps involved in the creative process: *Milk, Meet, Mist, Mull,* and *Map.*[5]

- **Milk**—Milk a lot of cows, but churn your own butter. "Original thinking is seldom original; it just looks that way. . . . I milk all the ideas I can from others. I read, study, interview, inspect, dissect, and observe. I take classes and endure seminars, I subscribe and ascribe, describe and transcribe, gathering premium ideas wherever possible."

"You are the same today that you are going to be in five years from now except for two things: the people with whom you associate and the books you read."[6]

When you think, hear, or see a worthwhile idea, write it down immediately. Keep a notebook in your car and paper on the nightstand. Ideas have a way of striking and then quickly vanishing. Ideas you get from other people vanish quickly as well. Write them down, file them, or throw them in a box for future reference. Someone said, "Opportunity is like a horse that gallops up and then pauses for a moment; if you don't get on, before long you hear the clatter of hoofbeats dying away in the distance." Ideas are like that—they come to you, then quickly disappear if not caught by pen and paper. How many times have you been in a meeting or somewhere and a wonderful thought comes to your mind? By the time you get home and are ready to record that thought, you cannot remember what it was.

Taking someone else's idea and using it without adapting it can lead to a disastrous result. Personalize a borrowed idea. Make it your own. It has to become a part of you before it will be successful for you.

- **Meet**—"Having milked all the available cows, the next step is to gather the butter-makers into one room for brainstorming, a time when we gather around the table with our pails of milk and start splashing each other. We suspend criticism and toss around ideas capriciously."

Ideas create ideas. Brainstorming with other people stimulates our own thinking. Proverbs 27:17 puts it this way. "As iron sharpens iron, so one man sharpens another."

- **Mist**—"The brainstorming process usually ends in the fabulous frustration of too many ideas.... A thick mental mist descends.... Now what? What do I do with all this stuff? What direction do I take? What application do I make? . . . It's like fighting through a corridor thick with cobwebs."

Having a variety of ideas is great, but determining which idea is the best to use can be a big decision to make, perhaps bigger than finding an idea in the first place. That's why it's like a mist—the right way ahead is not clearly defined.

- **Mull**—"Ideas must incubate for a while before they're hatched. They must wander through the chambers of the mind before they're ready for debut."

Morgan tells us that the mulling step consists of two main ingredients: prayer and getting away. Do something to get away from it for a period of time. Go for a walk. Take a break.

"That's why I almost always stall for time when. . . confronted with a problem, a need, or an aspiration. Sometimes we want to milk another's ideas and jump immediately to implementation. . . . make snap judgments on big issues. That's seldom wise . . . for 'a prudent man giveth thought to his steps' (Proverbs 14:15, KJV)."

- **Map**—Somewhere along the line we have to take an "idea and do the hard work of working out the details of implementation."

Obviously, these strategies require some advance thinking. This can be difficult for those who think best under pressure. But even pressure can be used to an advantage. Often the night before some deadline, the most wonderful thoughts will occur as to how something could be done. However, there is one terrible problem: time prohibits the implementation of those ideas. Grabbing one or two of these thoughts and implementing them in a haphazard manner can have a measure of success, but not to the greatest measure possible.

Principles of the Creative Process

Just as principles set in motion the harvest process, so principles are involved in the creative process.

USING OUR TALENTS

God has given us the ability to think, to reason, and to choose. He expects us to develop these gifts and to use them wisely. The Parable of the Talents refers to the stewardship of all the resources we have been given (Matthew 25). We are to be wise stewards, using and increasing the natural abilities God has given to each of us, whether we are one-, two-, or ten-talent people.

A gifted musician does not just sit down at the piano one day and begin to play difficult themes. It takes years of practice and honing of skills to develop his or her natural talents. It is the same with our creativity. As we use what we have, we become more creative. When we do not use it, we lose what we do have. "'Everyone who has will be given more, and he will have an abundance. Whoever does not have, even what he has will be taken from him'" (Matthew 25:29).

In his book *A Whack on the Side of the Head,* Roger von Oech says

> Some people stifle their creativity because they think that creativity belongs only to the Einsteins, Curies, and Shakespeares of the world. To be sure, these are some of the super luminaries of the creative firmament, but these people didn't get their big ideas right out of the blue. Most of their big ideas came from paying attention to their intermediate-sized ideas, working with them, and transforming them into big ideas. This is true for most intermediate-sized ideas. They come from small ideas which their creators paid attention to, and gradually worked into bigger things.[7]

We may not be a ten-talent person when it comes to creativity, but God would like to take our one or two talents and increase them to two or three. We must be willing to work with Him. Howard Hendricks states, "Nothing is more common than unfulfilled potential."[8]

GETTING IDEAS

Ralph W. Harris wrote, "God began with an idea when He created the universe. Every advance since then has begun the same way—the discovery of the Americas, invention of radio and television, landing on the moon—each began with an idea. We come the closest to the creativity of God when we get a worthwhile idea. Every achievement begins with an idea."[9]

In the business world nearly one out of three companies offers creativity training for its employees. Increasing numbers of universities are offering degrees in creative training. Experts call creativity the survival skill of the '90s. How much more important for the church not to limit itself to the ways it has always done things.

As Christians, we have an added benefit over the world. We can tap into the Source of unlimited ideas. An impression may come so strongly to our hearts that we know God has given us a divine inspiration. However, if the only ideas we use are the ones that came to us in that manner, we will accomplish very few things in our lives. Most of the time God uses natural processes to enable us to open our minds to what we should do. That is what we are doing in this study course—exposing ourselves to new ideas.

Agatha Christie, the famous British author of mysteries writes: "The first question put to an author . . . is: 'Where do you get your ideas from?'" She goes on to state

> The temptation is great to reply: "I always go to Harrods," or "I get them mostly at the Army and Navy Stores. . . . Try Marks and Spenser." The universal opinion seems firmly established that there is some magic source of ideas which authors have discovered how to tap. . . . If one idea in particular seems attractive, and you feel you could do something with it, then you toss it around, play tricks with it, work it up, tone it down, and gradually get it into shape. Then, of course, you have to start writing it. That is not nearly such fun—it becomes hard work. Alternately, you can tuck it carefully away in storage, for perhaps using in a year or two years' time.[10]

This process works not only for an author coming up with ideas for a new story line, but describes a procedure we can use to come up with ideas that will work in our ministries.

We can store ideas in a "Next Time I Do This, I Will Do It Like This" file. Some ideas that may have been used rather poorly the first time around can be pulled out, polished up, changed a little, and used in a better way another time.

Likewise, after a particular ministry event is over, you can think of many things you wish you would have thought to do or say. Do the same thing with those thoughts; write them down, and pull them out for use if you ever do anything remotely similar to what was just done.

Dreaming of Possibilities

In our early years of pastoring, my wife and I would go out for breakfast every Monday morning and talk about a variety of issues. Part of that time was spent dreaming and planning for the church and community where we felt the Lord had placed us.

We would begin these dreaming times by asking questions similar to these: What could we do to build our Sunday night services? What could we do to get the people who are starting to come to church into Sunday school? How could we best touch this community? What things could we do that would appeal to the unsaved? How could we reach new teens for the youth group? What could we do to improve the church nursery?

We set the following guideline for these sessions: We could feel free to list any idea, no matter how ridiculous, how far out, how impossible financially, or how limiting our facilities might be to using that idea. Neither of us were allowed to say at that time, "That will not work!" "That's the stupidest idea I ever heard of!" "We can't do that!" "We can't afford that!" "We don't have the resources to do that." These comments were probably applicable to most of our ideas. But by not using them at that particular time, we were not stymied in our thinking. We were able to break out of rigid thinking patterns.

Expanding the Dream

After listing all the ideas we could come up with, we would go home and think about them, let them settle, and pray over them. We would ask ourselves these questions: "Is there anything we have thought of that would work in some way? Could we change or alter any of these thoughts so it would become the right thing? Is there something we haven't thought of that should be added?"

At a later meeting, perhaps the next week or even the next

month, we would pick up that list, add to it, and alter it. We would circle anything that seemed particularly interesting or feasible to try in some area. Sometimes we would pick only a part of an idea. Time after time, we would find that either the Lord had raised up a leader in that area or a door would open where we could take steps to move in some direction with one of those ideas. Probably most of those ideas were never used. But some of them served as stepping-stones for other possibilities. Some ideas were discarded. Others were placed in a "Someday We'd Like To" file.

This process will work well in any area of church ministry. Following this formula allows vision to be expanded by lifting thinking above the present circumstances and enabling you to see beyond them.

1. Identify the project to be worked on.
2. Ask appropriate questions relevant to the particular task. (What could we do? How could this be improved?)
3. List every idea mentioned, no matter how foolish.
4. Let the ideas settle for a period of time.
5. Pray and think about the ideas.
6. Add any additional thoughts to the list.
7. Note particularly attractive and possible ideas; build on some, store others away for future use.

Throughout this process, pray, "Lord, think through me. Open my eyes. Help me see the potential and the possibilities. Is this the direction You want us to go?"

The principles that had been working for years in our lives were the basic principles that those who teach creative thinking courses suggest implementing. We had simply added the dimension of prayer.

Increasing the Probability of Success

In his article titled "Handing Your Baby to Barbarians," Craig Brian Larson states, "[When] we develop a creative idea, it becomes our baby, the most wonderful, beautiful, intelligent, and promising child ever to grace the earth. However, the time . . . arrives for proud parents to bring that brainchild into public, and that can be traumatic."[11] He gives several suggestions for increasing the chance of success for new ideas.

- "Keep it simple. . . . If people ever get the idea something is complex or beyond them, many won't even try. . . .
- "Be realistic about commitment. . . . Ask someone to babysit your brainchild . . . a few minutes, and there's a good chance they'll agree. But ask them to adopt her, support her from their own means, and promise to send her to a private college, and you'll have far fewer volunteers. . . .
- "Remember your parental bias. . . . No one adores our high concepts . . . as much as we do. We usually believe God inspired the idea. We felt the concept grow in the womb, labored to give her birth, nursed and cared for her in the middle of the night."[12]

No one is likely to care for your idea more than you do. Others must be inspired to buy into our ideas for them to work. Our ideas will have a greater chance of success as people learn to trust us. Trust must be earned, and earning trust involves time.

We can also increase an idea's chance of succeeding by testing it, using appropriate timing, and freeing people to not support it if they so choose.

Testing New Ideas

Try an idea for a short period of time or with a small group before you implement it or set something in motion churchwide for eternity. Then you will not be locked into programs that do not work. People are more likely to try something new if they know they do not have to do it forever.

While we were pastoring, our church grew enough to make it necessary to initiate two services to accommodate those attending. That was a frightening prospect for some of the people. They were afraid they would lose that small-church feeling of knowing everyone (which is what happened). But they bought into the idea of trying it for three months to see how it worked. By the end of three months, everyone liked it so much that we continued it and for a time even ran three services. This would have been difficult and would have caused needless frustration if we had started it as a forever project over the objections of many people rather than as a three-month trial.

The question of manipulation comes up when dealing with this subject. *Manipulation* is "stepping on people to get your ideas across." *Leadership* is "waiting for God to open the doors to the ideas you feel He has given you." John Maxwell tells us, "Leaders manipulate others when they move them for the leader's advantage. Leaders motivate others when they move them for everyone's advantage."[13]

TIMING

There is a time to present new ideas and a time to wait. Timing is crucial. Some ideas are lost because they are presented or discarded before their time. Another day, another way, or another need will surface for using a good idea.

Abraham was given a fantastic dream of fathering a nation, but when it did not occur in his timing, he developed his own creative idea, Ishmael. Even when Isaac, the son of promise, was born, he was asked to lay that dream on the altar (Genesis 12,16,22).

As a young man, Joseph had a fantastic dream of becoming a great ruler. However, for a long period in his life it looked as if that dream was an absolute impossibility. Yet, in God's time it did happen (Genesis 37 through 45).

David had a dream of building a house for God but was not allowed to complete that task. That did not mean the dream was not from God. David showed the spirit we need to have when we are not allowed to accomplish what we may have dreamed. David gathered all the material in preparation for his son, Solomon, to build the temple (2 Chronicles 6:7; 7:11).

FREEDOM FROM OBLIGATION

We must give people "the opportunity not to take part in a program without feeling guilty. By giving people a loophole, they can accept the existence of a program without feeling obliged to get involved or attend. When people do not feel an obligation to a new program, they will not try to attack it or to kill new ideas. But if they are not given a loophole, they will feel guilty and intimidated and will try to kill this new ministry."[14]

If our ideas did not work in the time and in the way we thought they should, let us determine not to allow that experience to keep us from trying again. Edison failed thousands of times before he succeeded with the light bulb.

Thoughts and ideas are possible that will revolutionize our lives and our ministries. These ideas will come to us in a variety of ways. Some will be developed through the disciplined use of our God-given creativity, some will be quickened to our hearts as we learn from others, and some God will drop into our hearts as we seek Him for effective ways of touching our world.

May we hear God speaking to our hearts regarding His direction for our ministries, "'This is the way; walk in it'" (Isaiah 30:21).

Endnotes

[1]Edward DeBono, *Six Thinking Hats* (Boston: Little, Brown and Company, 1985), passim.

[2]Rick Warren, *The Purpose Driven Church* (Grand Rapids, Mich.: Zondervan Publishing House, 1995), 87.

[3]George Bernard Shaw, quoted in Hans Finzel, *The Top Ten Mistakes Leaders Make* (Wheaton, Ill.: Victor Books, 1994), 195.

[4] George Barna, *Evangelism That Works* (Ventura, Calif.: Regal Books, 1995), 96, 104.

[5] Robert J. Morgan, "The Well-Fed Imagination," *Leadership Magazine,* Summer 1993, 30–33.

[6] Charles "Tremendous" Jones, quoted in John C. Maxwell, *Leadership 101* (Tulsa: Honor Books, 1994), 17.

[7] Roger von Oech, *A Whack on the Side of the Head* (New York: Warner Books, 1990), 165–66.

[8] Howard Hendricks, quoted in John C. Maxwell, *Leadership 101* (Tulsa: Honor Books, 1994), 96.

[9] Ralph W. Harris, "How to get ideas," *Advance,* March 1995, 22.

[10] Agatha Christie, *Passenger to Frankfurt* (New York: Harper Paperbacks, 1970), xi, xii.

[11] Craig Brian Larson, "Handing Your Baby to Barbarians," *Leadership Magazine,* Summer 1993, 46.

[12] Ibid., 46–47.

[13] John C. Maxwell, *Leadership 101* (Tulsa: Honor Books, 1994), 153.

[14] Paul Walker, "A Strategy for Innovation," *Ministries Today,* August 1991, 73.

8
Reaching This Generation

Striking out is an awful feeling! It is even worse in a championship game. You are the one standing at the plate with the score tied and the outcome of the game resting on your shoulders. The team and all the hometown fans are counting on you to hit the ball. The ball is thrown, you stand there holding the bat, but you don't swing. Then you hear those dreaded words, "Strike three! You're out!"

You probably remember the sinking sensation that comes in that kind of a situation or a similar one where it seems you failed everyone. The memories and feelings associated with those experiences seem to linger in our minds forever. No one enjoys striking out. We like to at least take a healthy swing at the ball.

One of the beginning principles a coach tries to teach is "If you want to hit the ball, you need to keep your eye on it." If we are to "hit the ball" as far as reaching our generation for Christ, we must keep our eyes on our target. Many times our focus as a church and as individuals is on everything but the task we are called to accomplish.

Our mission as believers is to reach this generation. This is not a choice; it is a mandate. We are in the redemption business.

Essentials for Our Mission

BEING AWARE OF NEEDS

Jesus said, "'Do you not say, "Four months more and then the harvest"? I tell you, open your eyes and look at the fields! They are ripe for harvest'" (John 4:35). The first step for reaching our generation successfully is to open our eyes to the opportunities around us. These opportunities often come disguised in the form of needs.

Needs are usually spotted easily, for they surround us. Newscasts and newspapers remind us of the needs in our nation and in our world. However, needs are not what drives us to action. Awareness of needs alone can numb us, overwhelm us, discourage us, and depress us. Needs can make us want to run away. Only when coupled with vision do needs serve as a catalyst for action. Vision allows us to look at a need and see that something can be done to bring about change.

LOVING THE LOST

When we care about people, we find a way to become involved in bringing change. When Nehemiah, who had been exiled, heard of the desperate situation in his hometown of Jerusalem, he "sat down and wept." He "mourned and fasted and prayed before the God of heaven" (Nehemiah 1:4).

The emotions we experience when thinking about those close to us being lost for eternity are but a small picture of the love that God has for every individual in the world. Our concern for lost people should extend beyond our immediate circle of family and friends.

God reminded Jonah of His care for all people. "'Nineveh has more than a hundred and twenty thousand people who cannot tell their right hand from their left, and many cattle as well. Should I not be concerned about that great city?'" (Jonah 4:11). God is "not wanting anyone to perish, but everyone to come to repentance" (2 Peter 3:9).

Love is the greatest of all motivations for harvest work. Love causes us to seek out appropriate ways of touching the people in our lives. Love—God's love through us—finds a way to reach the lost.

HAVING A VISION

In his book *Be All You Can Be,* John Maxwell, speaking of the importance of vision as a motivator, states:

> Tragically, our world is full of what I would call mundane men, people who see only what is immediate. They only reach out for things they can tangibly put their hands on. They go for the convenient. They never look beyond themselves, and they never look at what they could be. A mundane man may be a truck driver, a bank president, or a school teacher. Mundane men can be found in every profession. A mundane man is really someone who lacks depth because he lacks vision. The poorest person in the world is not the person who doesn't have a nickel. The poorest person in the world is the one who doesn't have a vision. If you don't have a dream—a goal and a purpose in life—you're never going to become what you could become.[1]

A vision has power. Our views dominate our lives. God is a God of vision. God gives people visions and dreams for a purpose. Here are visions given to the Early Church in the Book of Acts regarding the reaching of lost people:

Ananias received a vision. God told him to go pray for Saul of Tarsus. He was also told that Saul had received a vision of a man named Ananias coming to pray for him (Acts 9:10–12).

Cornelius had a vision. He was instructed to go to the home of Simon the tanner and ask for Peter, who would explain the things of God more fully to him. Peter also received a vision of the sheet coming down from heaven filled with unclean animals. This vision prepared Peter to minister to the Gentile, Cornelius (Acts 10).

Paul had a vision of a man standing and begging him,

"'Come over to Macedonia and help us'" (Acts 16:9).

While in Corinth, Paul had a vision regarding his ministry in that city: "'Do not be afraid; keep on speaking, do not be silent. For I am with you, and no one is going to attack and harm you, because I have many people in this city'" (Acts 18:9,10). Paul stayed in Corinth for a year and a half, teaching the people the Word of God.

Paul told King Agrippa that his Damascus Road experience occurred for the purpose of sending him to the Gentiles "to open their eyes and turn them from darkness to light, and from the power of Satan to God, so that they may receive forgiveness of sins" (Acts 26:18).

While we may or may not ever receive such dramatic vision experiences, God desires to birth His vision in each of us. Much of that vision will involve the rebuilding of human lives, or in Isaiah's words, the renewing of "the ruined cities that have been devastated for generations" (Isaiah 61:4).

Many plans and programs have been set in motion by people who were inspired by natural vision to solve the problems of this world. However, their efforts fall short because they deal with the symptoms, rather than with the root cause of those problems. Ezra Taft Benson's words remind us, "The Lord works from the inside out. The world works from the outside in. The world would take people out of the slums, Christ takes the slums out of people, and then they take themselves out of the slums. The world would mold men by changing their environment. Christ changes men, who then change their environment. The world would shape human behavior, but Christ can change human nature."[2]

Rebuilding of human lives cannot be accomplished by force. Someone once said, "A militant church is not a spiritual church. You cannot accomplish in the natural what can only be done in the supernatural."

The ruined cities and the devastation caused by cycles of abuse passed down through many generations can be truly changed only as people experience a change in their hearts.

This change of heart can take place as we open our eyes and our hearts to the need and allow God to breathe into us His vision and direction regarding that need.

Characteristics of Vision

In his book *Dying for Change,* Leith Anderson tells us that visions for God's work have the following characteristics:

1. Visions look to the future.
2. Visions see the way things could be.
3. Visions are in the eyes of leaders.
4. Visions drive us to action.[3]

VISION IS FORWARD LOOKING

The past is behind us. We can do nothing about it, other than to learn and build from it. The rest of our lives will be spent in the future. We can do something about that future.

Vision brings hope for tomorrow. Vision causes us to rise above our present circumstances. When God communicates vision to a human heart regarding a particular need it is awesome, for the person suddenly realizes that God is becoming involved in that situation. God's involvement means He desires to bring about some type of positive change.

VISION SEES POSSIBILITIES

Circumstances should not be allowed to dictate our vision. It is possible to find ourselves in wonderful circumstances with no vision. It is also possible to be filled with vision and hope even in difficult situations.

Some people worship in beautiful cathedrals and have all the resources needed to touch their world, but they have lost their vision for the lost. Other people, although imprisoned for their faith, have a strong grasp of a spectacular vision of people coming to salvation.

Vision Is Given to Leaders

Spiritual leaders are people of vision. They see what others do not see. They see problems as opportunities for God to work. They see lost people as future Christians.

Joshua and Caleb saw beyond the giants to the land of promise flowing with milk and honey. They said, "'We should go up and take possession of the land, for we can certainly do it'" (Numbers 13:30).

Hezekiah saw beyond the broken covenant with God to Israel's restoration of the covenant and return to God (2 Chronicles 29).

Nehemiah saw beyond the rubble of the broken and burnt walls of his hometown to the rebuilt, safe city of Jerusalem (Nehemiah 2).

Vision Is a Driving Force

Our vision dominates and drives our life. The very nature of vision implies action. "Martin Luther envisioned a reformed church and was driven to bring about the Reformation. John Knox had a vision of an evangelized Scotland and set about winning his nation to Christ and the church."[4]

Vision brings motivation to our lives. Charles Swindoll tells of a man who ardently admired Theodore Roosevelt and "once exclaimed to him, 'Mr. Roosevelt, you are a great man!' In characteristic honesty he replied, 'No, Teddy Roosevelt is simply a plain, ordinary man—highly motivated.' It is safe to say that his answer describes most great leaders . . . plain and ordinary, *yet highly motivated.*"[5]

Vision Is Contagious

Have you noticed when you get together with people of vision how it sparks vision in your own life? Or how hearing a message on vision generates vision in your life? Or consider the influence that one individual who is excited about a particular project or event has on those around him or her. The great leaders of history have all been able to inspire others by their vision. Rick Warren reminds us, "[P]eople respond to passionate vision, not need."[6]

VISION REQUIRES FOCUS

Accomplishing our vision requires focusing on our task. All sorts of things can come into our lives and diminish our vision. Vision can fade, blur, and sometimes even die.

Good things can crowd out the best things in our lives. Life can become so busy that we lose our focus and purpose for the task at hand.

Difficulties can blur our vision. Have you noticed all the things that enter into the mix whenever any work for God is started? Rarely are we allowed to concentrate totally on the task at hand.

Weariness can cause our vision to fade and discouragement can kill it. When we are physically and spiritually exhausted, we are vulnerable to discouragement. We need to care for the physical and spiritual needs of our lives so we do not become discouraged and lose heart.

We need to be aware that the enemy will try to keep us from accomplishing any vision God gives us. Discouragement and confusion are two of his main tools to stop the work of God. Being alert and aware of his tactics allows us to take appropriate action to guard against him. The apostle Paul warned the Corinthians to forgive an offense "in order that Satan might not outwit us. For we are not unaware of his schemes" (2 Corinthians 2:11).

Our vision is to obey God's mandate to bring lost people to Him. Occasionally, we may need to adjust our spiritual field glasses to regain a proper focus on the harvest. We must not allow our vision to fade, to become blurred, or to be altogether lost.

VISION REQUIRES PERSEVERANCE

Perseverance is "keeping on keeping on." It is sticking with a task even when it may appear that nothing is happening. Perseverance is necessary because a vision from God involves His timing.

Habakkuk received a vision and was told that the "revelation awaits an appointed time; it speaks of the end and will not prove false. Though it linger, wait for it; it will certainly come and will not delay" (Habakkuk 2:3). The problem would be solved at a future time, but it awaited God's appointed time.

We rarely receive an immediate reward for our labor. Evangelism is a process involving sowing, watering, and reaping. Scripture is very clear that the rewards go only to those who persevere. "Let us not become weary in doing good, for at the proper time we will reap a harvest if we do not give up" (Galatians 6:9). Robert Schuller put it this way, "Most people who succeed in the face of seemingly impossible conditions are people who simply don't know how to quit."[7]

Rick Warren illustrates the principle of perseverance by telling of the growth of the Chinese bamboo tree.

> Plant a bamboo sprout in the ground, and for four or five years (sometimes much longer) nothing happens! You water and fertilize, water and fertilize, water and fertilize—but you see no visible evidence that anything is happening. Nothing! But about the fifth year things change rather dramatically. In a six-week period the Chinese bamboo tree grows to be a staggering ninety feet tall! *World Book Encyclopedia* records that one bamboo plant can grow three feet in a single twenty-four hour period. It seems incredible that a plant that lies dormant for years can suddenly explode with growth, but it happens without fail with bamboo trees.[8]

Warren goes on to give this advice to pastors, and we could apply it to all church ministries: "Don't worry about the growth of your church. Focus on fulfilling the purposes of your church. Keep watering and fertilizing and cultivating and weeding and pruning."9 We often concentrate on the wrong things. God will take care of the growth of our ministries if we concentrate on the right things and persevere.

Vision Can Be Disobeyed

Knowing and doing are two different things. Paul, speaking of the vision he had received on the Damascus Road, told King Agrippa that he "'was not disobedient to the vision from heaven'" (Acts 26:19). Like Paul, we need to be faithful to the vision and direction that God puts in our hearts.

Vision Requires Testing

A word of caution must be considered here. Vision needs to be tested. "Do not believe every spirit, but test the spirits to see whether they are from God" (1 John 4:1).

A vision from God will not lead us contrary to the principles of the Word of God. A vision from God will usually be confirmed by godly counsel. A vision from God stands the test of time; it can wait for God's timing.

Vision Requires Prayer

In Nehemiah 1 through 6, we can learn much from how Nehemiah carried out the vision God had placed in his heart for the rebuilding of the walls of Jerusalem. Nehemiah prayed at every step along the way. He prayed initially upon hearing of the need, prayed while waiting for the opportunity to speak to the king regarding the need, prayed upon encountering each of the many obstacles that came to stop him. Prayer is our greatest resource. Prayer is the key that will open our eyes and ears to hear what God would have us to do in regard to the need.

Prayer must be a part of the beginning, middle, and end of all harvest work. Prayer will help us rise above all difficulties.

It will enable us to keep focused on the need to reach this generation.

George Barna reminds us that a "church that strives to evangelize its community without saturating its efforts in prayer is like a race car driver that jumps into his car at the starting line and discovers that the tank has not been filled with gasoline. We cannot hope to influence the hardened hearts and stray souls of humankind without inviting God to empower and bless our meager efforts on His behalf."[10]

Ministering to This Generation

The great heroes of faith were men and women of God who served their generation. At some point in their lives, they became aware that they were God's men and women placed in their generation in God's time for God's purposes. Mordecai asked Esther, "'Who knows but that you have come to royal position for such a time as this?'" (Esther 4:14). She was the person placed in a position in that generation to save the Jewish people from death.

Perhaps the greatest thing that could be said of any of us is what is said of David in the Book of Acts: "'When David had served God's purpose in his own generation, he fell asleep'" (Acts 13:36).

A Unique Generation

Rick Warren comments: "The fact is, we can't serve God in any other generation except our own. Ministry must always be done in the context of the current generation and culture. We must minister to people in the culture as it really is—not in some past form that we may have idealized in our minds. We can benefit from the wisdom and experiences of great Christian leaders who lived before us but we cannot preach and minister the way they did because we don't have the same culture."[11]

Every generation has had its own unique challenges. This

generation is no exception. Reaching the people of our generation may require us to walk down paths we have never walked before.

Leith Anderson, quoting the Win Arn Growth Report, gives us some helpful insight regarding touching this generation. This information contrasts styles of evangelism which he calls "old paradigms" and "new paradigms."[12]

Effective Evangelism	
Confrontational	Relational
Mass	Personal
General Population	Specific "people groups"
Single Presentation	Multiple exposure
Single Method	Multiple methods
Goal: a decision	Goal: a disciple
America: a Christian nation	America: a secular mission field
Church membership	Church discipleship
Motive: guilt	Motive: value & love

TOOLS FOR THIS GENERATION

We need to remember that God has always given His people all they have needed to accomplish His work. The Early Church had none of the technology or resources available today, but they were able to reach their generation with the gospel.

God has given us the tools we need to reach this world.

Consider how He has provided for us....

- To defuse our fears, He promises ultimate victory.
- To encourage our hearts, He provides glimpses of that victory while it is still in progress.

- To shore up our weaknesses, He provides His strength through the working of the Holy Spirit within and through us.
- To enhance our natural capabilities, He provides special gifts and fellow believers whose gifts complement ours.
- To sharpen our minds, He has provided all types of technology, data and analytic tools to understand and reach our world.
- To provide us with direction, He has left us His Word, which contains the principles we need to achieve personal holiness, corporate significance and eternal impact.[13]

When we do our part, God does more than His part.

EVANGELIZING THIS GENERATION

Though we are faced with a great challenge, we are part of a great army that is scattered across the nation and around the world. Every community and most neighborhoods in America contain a Christian influence. Imagine what could happen if all Christians simply took responsibility for at least praying (preparing the ground) for the part of world that is right in front of them. That prayer should include that God would draw, soften, and bring people into their lives that they could influence toward Christ.

If each of us simply started at that point, the other steps would follow. Love for those around us would flood into our hearts, providing the motivation to find the right ways of touching those individuals. We would become aware of doors of opportunity open to us. God would give us a new sensitivity to the Holy Spirit's leading in our lives and show us how to effectively reach this generation. He would provide the same basic ingredients it has always taken to reach lost people of every generation—love, vision, and desire.

George Barna sums it all up in saying that in his study of effective evangelism he had been "snared by one of the seductive but erroneous notions promoted in our culture: To be on the cutting edge, something has to be newer, bigger, flashier, more complex. Also erroneous is the belief that the future will be dominated by those people who are the most innovative. To be the best, they will have to be the most unusual, the most creative, the most energetic, the biggest risk-takers."[14]

We do not need new models for evangelism. We need to understand the technology and the heart and passion Jesus exemplified for us in His ministry. We must be aware of the people we are called to reach, true to scriptural principles, and committed to reaching people with the love of Christ through personal commitment and perseverance.

Innovation did not bring the tremendous revivals that occurred throughout history; radical obedience to the call to evangelize brought the revivals. Evangelism is effective when people do whatever is necessary to reach the unchurched of their generation, rather than maintain traditions and accept outdated assumptions. Effective evangelism is not about programs, methods, or techniques. It is about people who love Christ and love other people in the name of Christ.

Nike uses a promotional slogan that should be the Church's evangelistic motto: "Just do it!"

Endnotes

[1] John C. Maxwell, *Be All You Can Be* (Wheaton, Ill.: Victor Books, 1987), 51.

[2] Ezra Taft Benson, quoted in Stephen R. Covey, *The 7 Habits of Highly Effective People* (New York: A Fireside Book, 1989), 309.

[3] Leith Anderson, *Dying for Change* (Minneapolis: Bethany House Publishers, 1990), 168–71.

[4] Ibid., 171.

[5] Charles Swindoll, *Hand Me Another Brick* (Nashville: Thomas Nelson, Inc., 1978), 18.

[6] Rick Warren, *The Purpose Driven Church* (Grand Rapids: Zondervan Publishing House, 1995), 345.

[7] Robert Schuller, quoted in John C. Maxwell, *Leadership 101* (Tulsa: Honor Books, 1994), 41.

[8]Warren, *The Purpose Driven Church,* 393, 394.

[9]Ibid., 394.

[10]George Barna, *Evangelism That Works* (Ventura, Calif.: Regal Books, 1995), 128.

[11]Warren, *The Purpose Driven Church,* 396.

[12]Win Arn Growth Report, quoted in Leith Anderson, *A Church for the 21st Century* (Minneapolis: Bethany Books, 1992), 150.

[13]George Barna, *Today's Pastor* (Ventura, Calif.: Regal Books, 1993), 168.

[14]George Barna, *Evangelism That Works,* 96.